MAYDAY

MAYDAY

MAYDAY
A Comeback Story

ANGIE WELTY

Cherish
EDITIONS

First published in Great Britain 2021 by Cherish Editions
Cherish Editions is a trading style of Shaw Callaghan Ltd & Shaw
Callaghan 23 USA, INC.
The Foundation Centre
Navigation House, 48 Millgate, Newark
Nottinghamshire NG24 4TS UK
www.triggerhub.org
Text Copyright © 2021 Angie Welty

British Library Cataloguing in Publication Data
A CIP catalogue record for this book is available upon request
from the British Library
ISBN: 9781913615277
This book is also available in the following eBook formats:
ePUB: 9781913615161
Angie Welty has asserted her right under the Copyright,
Design and Patents Act 1988 to be identified as the author of this work
Cover design by Kitty Turner
Typeset by Lapiz Digital Services

AUTHOR BIO

Angie Welty lives with her husband in the beautiful Pacific Northwest in a small town called Boring outside Portland, Oregon.

She has two grown children, Cody and Dana. In her spare time, Angie loves to run, bike, and spend time with her friends and large extended family.

She is in her happy place when she has her toes in the sand, the sun on her face, and her family nearby.

To the man who saved my son's life, to the mental health professionals and doctors who helped him recover, and to my family

CONTENTS

FOREWORD

When Angie asked me to write a foreword to her book, I didn't hesitate. She and her family have experienced at first hand the results of a mental health trauma and what can happen when it goes undiagnosed and untreated. It was through my relationship with Cody that I grew closer to Angie and her family. Our paths began to cross more frequently as we navigated the complexity of youth suicide prevention awareness, though on different paths.

I began my mental health career as a staff member in a psychiatric residential treatment facility for youth in Portland, Oregon. After earning my Masters of Social Work degree, I went on to become a therapist for children and families. I frequently saw clients who experienced depression and were formally diagnosed with this condition. It was not uncommon for me to make a recommendation for a youth to be seen in the emergency room for further assessment because of acute suicidality and concern for safety.

Even though I had years of mental health education, I was missing one crucial piece – suicide prevention training. It wasn't until approximately five years ago that I learned that suicide is the second leading cause of death for young people aged between 10 and 24 years. Nor was it until that time that I learned that the risk of suicide is significant after discharge from a psychiatric unit or from an emergency room (for behavioral health-related issues). In 2019, 47,511 suicide deaths occurred in the US.

Six years ago the organization I work with became intentional about suicide prevention, and I was hired as the suicide prevention coordinator to lead this crucial initiative. To introduce this new role to the community and as a way to take the temperature of our community's willingness to talk about suicide, we held a youth suicide prevention summit that included a panel of experts. The voice of lived experience is crucial and, in preparation for the summit, I set my sights on finding a young person who identified as a suicide-attempt survivor and who would be willing to share their experience in front of an audience (it resulted in being an audience of nearly 200). During this search, I was referred to Cody by a school district communications director.

Cody and I began email and text exchanges. After Cody agreed to participate, we decided to meet in person over coffee to discuss the summit event in more detail. It didn't take long into our conversation about his story before I realized that this young college student would be an important voice on mental health for our community education. Cody shared intimate details of his story, what led up to his attempt and his path to recovery. He spoke of the stigma that surrounds mental health and the difficulties he experienced in speaking openly about what was later determined to be a diagnosis of depression. A shared passion for mental health education has created a lasting friendship and bond between us.

History has shown that action by organizations can, eventually, make a large and life-saving difference, even for issues that at first seem impossible. In the last 70 years, tremendous strides have been made in the fight against cancer, HIV/AIDS, stroke, polio, smallpox and other diseases; as a result, mortality rates have decreased. In the case of suicide, we have yet to be intentional and we have yet to make this a priority.

We know from data who is at risk for suicide. We know about protective and risk factors, we have universal screening tools available to us, evidence-based and promising practices for gatekeeper training, risk formulation development and various treatments for suicidality. What remains is actually committing to doing this work and giving as many resources and finances to suicide prevention as we have for other public health issues. Until we create a system that supports this work as a priority, countless lives will continue to be lost.

This book is a critical support tool for parents, teachers, young people, coaches, families and those affected by the results of mental health trauma. It shines a light on our society's inability to normalize mental health. Until we have a system in place that makes suicide prevention a priority and a system where talking about mental health is done just as easily and openly as talking about our physical health, books like *Mayday* should be required reading for all of us.

Galli Murray, LCSW
Suicide Prevention Coordinator

PREFACE

I never intended to make public what began as journal entries written in fear, panic and desperation. They were just for me; my way of making sense of a living nightmare. At some point, the need to tell my story outweighed the need to keep private the unimaginable. Even before writing the first chapter, I knew in my heart how powerful the story would be, how each word would pour out of me.

When my son asked me to help him help others not go down his painful path, I felt the agony of his pain. His most desperate hour had become mine too, and I mustered the courage and placed my faith in the story of hope.

I want to give you hope, even if it is just a string that you are holding onto. I needed that string too. For so long, I tried to find something to read that would give me hope as I was crumbling inside. I was looking for any answers or a step-by-step guide to lead me through the maze I was in. I don't have all the answers, but maybe by sharing my story you will not feel alone in yours. You may even avoid some of the missteps, or you may take away some ideas that could work for you. I know without a doubt that the more we talk about mental illness the more we can do to shed the darkness and fear around this taboo subject. I want more light to be created through education, truth and hope. It is a common feeling to fear the unknown. I'd change the phrase "mental illness" if I could as so many react in fear to those words; that was also my first reaction. But I have hope for treatment, hope for recovery and hope for healing.

Trauma has a way of affecting your memory, so some of my recollection may not be perfect. I have done my best to be as accurate as possible by conducting research and talking to many of those personally involved in our story, to not only verify my journal notes but to get their recollection of events.

The story you're about to read embodies every emotion imaginable, to depths I could never have foreseen. As you read my words in these pages, my greatest desire is that they help you heal and not fear a diagnosis of mental illness. Fear wants to paralyze you; don't let it. If this book gives you more confidence to talk with your loved ones about their mental health and wellbeing then I've accomplished my mission. Let's all be the messengers of HOPE and recovery.

Welcome to my story.

1
THE CALL

*It's a story of sadness, it's a story of hope and most
importantly, it's a story of recovery.*
Cody Welty

"Mrs Welty, I need to know you're hearing me." I *was* hearing
the Deputy's voice on the other end, but I couldn't actually take
in what he was saying. I leaned against the kitchen counter to
support myself as the words "suicide attempt" came through
the phone line, instantly shattering my comfortable reality.
What the hell was happening? How did I miss this? He must be
talking about someone else's son. But he wasn't. What started
off as a beautiful first day of May in 2013 ended up being the
longest, darkest hours that forever changed the trajectory of
my family's lives and all of those around us. How we got here
was not your typical path to crisis, or so I thought.

My husband Will and I met in college and became engaged
in our final year. We were married in March 1991. Cody came
along in 1995 at a roaring 9lb and 10oz. His sister Dana followed
almost four years later at a smaller 8lbs, 10oz. We had our family
and I couldn't have been happier. I loved being a mom, and
Will was an involved, loving father. When the children were
young, we moved to a little town called Boring. There we built
our home and were fortunate enough to be part of a close-knit

community of family and friends who loved and cared for each other. Our time over the years was spent watching, supporting and coaching our children in their varied activities. When we could get away, we enjoyed travelling to see family out of state, or camping, inner tubing and skiing at Prineville Reservoir with family and friends.

Life was moving at warp speed. One morning I blinked and Cody was a junior in high school and Dana was in her last year of middle school. The year was 2013. I felt good about my relationship with my children. It took work, but I felt our family was strong. As I was coasting along, enjoying the ride, something was happening within my family that I didn't see or wasn't aware of. A storm was coming – the clouds were closing in, the thunder was about to roar and lightning would strike.

Wednesday, May 1st, 2013, started off as any other day. I could hear the kids upstairs getting ready for school, those sounds that become familiar with everyday life. Once they both got downstairs, we discussed the upcoming day and chatted about what they wanted for dinner; I knew it would need to be simple because Cody had a home baseball game that night. We agreed on chicken and rice. Cody then headed out early to meet a friend at Starbucks before class. Dana gathered her backpack, and we loaded into my car. I would drop her off and head into work. At the time, I was transitioning into the role of General Manager at a local fitness club. My work schedule that day included a department head meeting and individual meetings with staff that might run late. I wanted to be done in time for Cody's 4:30pm baseball game, ideally with enough time to watch warm-ups, which I'd always enjoyed.

Baseball had always been Cody's passion, and he pursued the sport he loved with time, energy and talent. In most areas involving school and sports, Cody excelled. He was a student leadership team member, a multi-sport varsity letterman athlete in baseball, football and racquetball, all while maintaining excellent grades. Cody was a sensitive soul and always eager to please. Never would I have thought those qualities, without the right balance, could become a burden.

I wrongly assumed that because Cody was actively involved in school and sports that he was happy. No one knew the tremendous amount of pain he was living with, not even me, his mother. Being completely honest, I thought I had this parenting thing down. I was wrong. I was naive. And I was to experience at first hand the pain of not knowing when your child is in crisis. I did not see what was coming.

It was a short drive from work to the baseball field. I planted myself in my usual seat in the bleachers to enjoy the game, but I sensed something was off with Cody. When he came up to bat, he didn't go through his normal sequence of steps. He seemed too casual, too matter-of-fact. I remembered thinking, "That seems strange." I placed that thought somewhere in my mind to bring up later. Dana, my 14-year-old, arrived and we finished watching the game. I saw Cody after the game and said, "We'll see you at home." The players had to stay to take care of the field after a home game, so I knew it would be a bit longer before he made it home for dinner.

I had picked up a rotisserie chicken for dinner. As I was prepping the rest of the meal, I texted Cody to remind him we were having dinner at home. Something strange happened – he didn't return my text. And Cody always returned my texts. I reasoned that it must be taking longer to take care of the field. Dana was upstairs watching a movie, and I needed to run over to my neighbor and best friend Nicole's house to wish her mother a happy birthday. Our kids grew up together, so Nicole and her husband Scott are like Cody and Dana's adopted parents. I decided to quickly walk next door and do that while I waited for Will to get home from work and Cody to come home. I took my phone with me. When I was there, I felt uncomfortable and anxious, wondering why Cody still hadn't texted or called. I told Nicole, "Hey, I'll be back, I need to check on why Cody isn't home yet."

When I got back home, Will had just walked through the door from work. I asked him if he had heard from Cody yet; he hadn't. I tried calling Cody and it went right to his voicemail. I looked at Will as I looked down at my phone shaking my head. Something was wrong. It shouldn't have gone straight to voicemail. I racked my brain trying to remember if he had a leadership meeting or a team thing going on after the game. Worry turned to fear. I called my friend, Jenni, whose son Mitchell was Cody's friend and on the same baseball team, to see if Mitchell was home, but it went straight to voicemail. I looked straight at Will with my heart pounding. "If I don't hear from him in 15 minutes, I'm calling out the cavalry. Something is wrong." We both sat down at the dinner table looking at each other in silence. I had never felt anything like this before. I was trying to convince myself that nothing was wrong, yet knew something was. Within minutes my gut feeling turned into a horrendous reality as our landline phone rang. I just knew it was going to be bad news.

The man on the other end of the line said, "Is this Mrs Welty?"

"Yes," I replied.

"Mrs Welty, I am a Deputy Sheriff for Clackamas County."

"Okay," I said. Questions began to pile up in my mind, but I waited for him to continue.

"I'm with your son Cody and I first want to tell you he is physically okay, but there has been a situation," he said.

My heart was pounding so hard, my chest tightened. My gaze was glued to my husband. "I don't understand. Was he in an accident?" *What did he mean, Cody was okay?* I was getting more agitated by the second.

"Mrs Welty, the paramedics are with your son now. He is breathing well," said the Deputy.

At that point my voice rose and I asked strongly, "I don't understand, was he in an accident?"

The Deputy proceeded with another question. He asked if I was aware of a particular location. I said, "Yes." I knew the road he was talking about. It didn't make sense for Cody to be there. I don't remember him telling me he was going anywhere after the game. What had I missed? Was there a study group going on at a friend's house? Is that why he was in that area the Deputy described? Is that why he hadn't answered my texts – because the reception in that area was not good? All these thoughts raced through my head. My husband kept looking at me for some reassurance of what was going on.

Then the Deputy's voice changed, slowed and he said, "Mrs Welty, I need to know you're hearing me."

"Yes, I am. What is going on?"

The Deputy then, in almost slow motion, said, "Mrs Welty, your son attempted suicide tonight. He is okay. He was saved by a cyclist."

I looked at Will, who had kept his eyes on me the entire time I was on the phone. He looked at me afraid. I muttered the words to him. He crumbled into himself and began to cry. My heart felt like it was being crushed. My body was physically reacting without any of my control. I could feel my body begin to shake. My legs felt like they could no longer support me. I could not speak.

The Deputy said, "Based on your reaction, I'm assuming you had no idea what was happening with Cody."

My head dropped in disbelief as I whispered, "No."

The Deputy proceeded to make the final statement that locked in the truth and seriousness of what he was telling me. "Mrs Welty, he left a note."

My son, my poor son. How did this happen? That was all I kept saying. So much pain, he must be in so much pain.

The Deputy was talking to me, but I couldn't tune him in. It was like being in a tunnel and the words sounded like echoes. I finally heard his voice come back into clarity as he was repeating the same statement. I don't know how many times he repeated himself.

"Mrs Welty, do you understand what I am saying?" he said insistently.

"Yes, yes," is all I could say. "How is he? Can I talk to him?" I asked.

The Deputy responded, "There is a firefighter here named John. He says he knows you, and he'd like to tell you how Cody is."

John said softly, "Angie, I can't imagine what you are feeling right now, but I wanted to tell you that Cody is physically okay. He is crying but his breathing is good."

At this point, I still didn't know exactly what had happened. If the Deputy had told me, I couldn't recall what he had said.

John continued to tell me that they wanted him transported in an ambulance to Portland Adventist Hospital, "The Deputy will meet you there."

I hung up the phone and collapsed on the floor. I was sick to my stomach. Will was trying to comfort me. I couldn't respond. We tried to talk to each other but it was all jumbled and I felt like I couldn't even hear correctly. We knew Dana was upstairs, but we didn't want to get her yet. I couldn't even make a decision. I called Nicole, sobbing as I tried to tell her about Cody. She raced over to our house with Scott. When she got here, I was shaking and could not compose myself. I asked if they would stay with Dana while we went to the hospital. I didn't want my daughter to see me in distress and I didn't know what to tell her. I couldn't get a grip. I still didn't know how Cody attempted it. I didn't have all the facts yet. I didn't want to scare Dana any more than she was going to be.

Scott offered to drive, but Will said he was okay to drive. Nicole gently walked me to our car.

I just kept saying, "I don't know how to do this."

She kept repeating, "You can do this, you can do this."

"Please tell Dana we don't know everything yet, and we will call for her when we know more," I said. Nicole hugged me and we drove away.

I have replayed that situation over in my head hundreds, if not thousands, of times, and I regret that decision to leave without trying to explain to Dana; during her time of fear, we weren't there for her.

The drive to the hospital was wrought with anxiety. I thought about a conversation with Cody two days before at dinner when he said he was in health class and they were going over the signs of depression. He confided how he felt he had some of those symptoms. I remember telling him that we would talk more about it after dinner. As we were all cleaning up after dinner, Cody sat on the corner of the kitchen counter and we discussed the idea that if he continued to feel he might be depressed, we could set up a counseling appointment.

I remember Cody asking me, "What would I say to a counselor?"

I said, "Whatever you feel you need to say." By the end of the chat, I followed up with, "If you keep feeling this way, we'll make an appointment."

He jumped off the counter and said, "I love you Mom", and headed up to his room. Even then, I never realized that Cody was doing so poorly emotionally that it would result in us driving to the hospital. I thought it was normal teenage hormones and growing pains. Nothing in his daily behavior made me think otherwise.

I could barely stomach reliving that after-dinner conversation. Oh my God, could I have stopped this? I was truly afraid, but not just one side of fear, every side: past, present and future were all rolling together and smothering me. Nothing made sense. I trembled as I tried to gain some source of understanding. I can't even tell you what Will and I talked about on the way, except that traffic wasn't going fast enough. One thought kept nagging me. How did I miss the signs? That thought led to others. Were there any signs to miss? What mother can't see this type of pain? I reminded myself we were a happy family. We didn't yell, we had family meals, we would encourage one another, I told my children I loved and supported them. Even with all those positive aspects, I had failed somehow. My brain couldn't keep up with all the thoughts pouring in at once. Memories and pictures of our life screamed through my mind. I wanted and needed answers.

As I brought my mind back to center, I called my sister Marita. Her husband Les answered and he could tell by my voice that something was wrong. He raced to give Marita the phone while she was in the shower. What I remember telling her is a blur; I just heard her say she was getting ready as fast as she could and would get to the hospital. The only other phone call I made was to Jenni, my friend who I had tried to call earlier, but it went to her voicemail. I needed her to know what happened. I wanted to know if her son Mitchell knew if something happened after the baseball game. I was begging for some answers from someone. The season had been a struggle; Cody was actually expressing a desire not to play ball his senior year. Jenni answered as I was still in mid-thought. I tried to stabilize my shaky voice, but she knew immediately something was wrong. I told her what had happened and she was in complete shock; she couldn't believe what she was hearing. She said she would talk to Mitchell and get back to me as soon as possible. Before we got off the phone, I asked her not to share this information with anyone else. Just as I hung up, my phone rang. It was the baseball coach.

Before I answered, I wondered why he was calling. Did he know what was happening right now? I answered and he just said my name and that he knew what was happening. I was so mad, I just yelled, "What happened tonight?"

He tried to calm me down and tell me, "Nothing, nothing happened."

I just couldn't believe that. I couldn't say anything else.

He said that they were on the way to the hospital, and all I could say was "Okay", before I hung up. I'm not sure why I thought it was okay for him to come, but I think I was hoping he would have some answers.

Will and I arrived at the hospital and I looked around. My sister Marita and her son, J.R., were already there. Marita looked at me and I could see in her eyes her own state of panic. Marita's husband Les and their daughter Courtney would arrive later. Courtney and Cody were only six weeks apart in age and grew up side by side. I had babysat Courtney on my days off during the week when I didn't work full time. She, Cody and Dana were extremely close. Marita's hair was wet, and I remembered that Les had had to get her out of the shower. I checked in at the ER desk and they said Cody hadn't arrived yet. I just stood there trying to take everything in.

Then my nephew, J.R., took me aside and said, "Angie, do you want to know what happened?" J.R. was a volunteer firefighter at the time, so he had access to some information.

I said, "Yes" because I still didn't even know exactly what Cody did.

J.R. proceeded to explain that Cody had tried to take his life by carbon monoxide poisoning. The EMTs chose this hospital because it had a barometric chamber that, if necessary, they could use. But, based on what J.R. knew, Cody was not exhibiting signs of needing that type of treatment.

Will and I just stood there in disbelief. With the new information, I couldn't sit down. I had to pace while processing.

I saw what I believed to be Cody's ambulance. All I wanted to do was see my son. But it would be another two hours before he was ready to see us.

2

THE ER

Once the ambulance arrived, I went to the emergency room desk where they confirmed it was Cody's; I did the paperwork to check Cody in, and they escorted Will and me to a private room. We were to wait until the Deputy arrived to meet with us; minutes later the door opened, and Will and I both jumped up to meet him.

The Deputy introduced himself and gently asked us to sit down. He must have seen the panicked look on our faces. It was as if he was trying to slow us down. He explained in more detail what had happened. On an iPad he showed us where they found Cody. While the Deputy's mouth moved, I waited for my brain to catch up. Yes, I would need this information eventually, but at that moment all I wanted was to see my son. As the Deputy continued to detail his findings regarding the evening, I struggled to process his words. Later, recounting with other people, and eventually Cody himself, allowed me to fully face the sequence of events and come to terms with them. Right then, I couldn't have repeated back any of what the Deputy was saying. Since I now know intimately the painful details, I can relay what happened in the room; however, at the time, I couldn't take on board all that was being thrown my way.

What the Deputy first told Will and me in that room was the story of the man who saved our son's life. On the road where Cody's car was hidden in the brush, a cyclist had gotten ahead of his wife and father-in-law, and he turned around to find them. Without realizing it, he had already passed Cody's car going one direction, but now pedaling in the opposite direction the cyclist glimpsed Cody's car in the brush and saw that something wasn't right. When he got to the car, he pulled Cody out. His wife caught up and flagged down a car, and asked them to call 911.

That was all the detail we received that night. But that was not the full story. Later, we would have the opportunity to hear the rest of the story directly from the man who saved our son's life. Right then, I understood this much: a miracle had happened.

The Deputy said that when he arrived at the scene, he found Cody weeping in the arms of the cyclist, "I can't even do that right...," Cody had cried.

The Deputy paused, his eyes softened and, with tenderness and compassion, he said, "I believe Cody was feeling overwhelmed and was unsure what to do."

Will and I had no words. The Deputy was describing a boy who didn't sound like our son. Cody didn't walk around sad. He laughed, joked and hugged. What did it mean that he felt overwhelmed?

How did I miss this? Did I let my child down? I loved our children more than I could ever express. I personally never felt love like I had for them. I learned from them what unconditional love looked like. I needed more information.

The Deputy handed us the folded note that Cody left. It felt heavy in my trembling hands. I slowly unfolded the note, terrified of what I would read on that paper. Will and I read in silence. His words, written in pencil, by his hand. Tears welled in my eyes. My head started to pound. I couldn't stop my tears. I cried harder than I thought humanly possible. My heart was throbbing in my chest. It was as if I could physically feel Cody's pain. I didn't know if I could handle the overwhelming emotions. I fought the feeling of desperation by focusing on the fact that our son was alive. We had a second chance. These would not be the last words from our son.

The Deputy left us his contact card and said to call if we needed anything.

A nurse came in and said Cody wasn't ready to see us yet, that he needed more time before he was ready. But she said we could write him a letter and she'd give it to him. She was so kind, I wondered what she thought of us – what type of parents must we be? My own fear chipped away at any confidence I had left in regard to being a parent and making decisions. I had been humbled below sea level.

During the few minutes she left us alone, Will and I just looked at each other. What should we say? I had one shot at making sure I told him he would be okay, that we were here, we were not upset and we loved him. We each wrote our own love letter to him on one sheet of paper. I folded it and prayed. *Please let him feel the love we have for him.*

The nurse returned and took our letter.

I looked at Will and said, "It's time for Dana to be here with us." We walked out to the waiting room to call her.

As I dialed our home number, I was still unsure what to reveal over the phone. When she answered, I conveyed that Cody had had a situation, but he was okay. I tried to calm her, but I recognized the panic in her voice. I assured her that Scott would bring her to us at the hospital now. I asked her to let me talk to Scott; she hollered downstairs to him to pick up the phone as she had answered the phone in our bedroom. She told me later that, when Uncle Scott picked up the phone downstairs, as she was placing the phone down she heard me tell him, "She doesn't know yet." I can't even imagine after hearing that what the drive must have been like for her – let alone the anger that she must have been feeling toward me for not telling her the whole situation over the phone. That would not be the only moment I wish I had a chance to redo.

I walked round the corner from the area in the ER that I had found to make the call from. Our family and friends in the waiting room were talking with each other until they noticed me, and then everyone stopped talking. I didn't want to talk to anyone. All I could think about was wanting Dana to get here. I needed my family together. I still didn't want to tell her what happened; I knew how painful it was going to be. It took about 25 minutes for Dana to arrive. The waiting made my anxiety build. In the meantime, a nurse came to inform us a social worker was talking to Cody. I then noticed she held a folded sheet of paper. She smiled and said, "Cody wrote you back." She led us into the same private waiting room and handed us the letter.

Seeing his handwriting again made me choke up. He was just down the hall, but I couldn't go to him yet. The letter gave us comfort, just knowing he had written back. We read that letter over and over again. It was my lifeline to him right now. I could see my son in those words. I could see hope. I folded the letter and kept it close to me. Now all I wanted was for Dana to arrive.

I took this opportunity to ask Wade, one of Cody's favorite teachers and a coach, how he and the baseball coach knew what had happened.

He said, "The car that was flagged down by the cyclist's wife happened to be the attendance secretary at the high school. She knows Cody and made calls to the Athletic Director, myself and the baseball coach."

That answered my question about why the coach had called me and had known what had happened. I was still missing information, but I had a piece of the puzzle. The rest would unfold over the next few days. I asked Wade to let the administration know that I wanted to keep this matter private until we knew more. I wanted to protect Cody and Dana. He completely agreed; only Cody's and Dana's school administrators would know.

I saw Scott's van pull into the parking lot, which meant Dana was finally here. I can still tell you exactly what she was wearing when she walked through those double automatic doors into the ER. Will and I were waiting for her by the door. She looked afraid and confused. I knew that what I was about to tell her would only add layers to each of those emotions. Will and I went to her and just hugged her. I tried to speak but the lump in my throat made it difficult for the words to come out. My throat was dry and raspy. Wade later told me that moment for him was the most painful to watch. We all knew Dana's world was going to be turned upside down and there was no way to soften the blow.

Will and I sat down with Dana and did our best to explain what happened. I didn't realize at the time that Dana could see Wade directly from where she was sitting and they were making eye contact. How I wish I had another chance to redo that moment and ask for a private room somewhere. Her downcast gaze met ours with increasing sorrow, and I could tell she was trying to process everything. It didn't help that I couldn't even say the word suicide. I kept mispronouncing it, maybe because I was scared to say it? She just wanted to know her brother was okay and wanted to see him. I told her that we didn't have a timeline for seeing him, and we just had to be patient.

A few minutes after we had updated Dana, a woman came to speak to Will and me. It was the social worker who had evaluated Cody. She sat down and asked if the people surrounding us were family. I said, "Yes, but also close friends." She asked if she could ask a couple of questions to all of us. It would help her with Cody's situation. Will and I were open to anything that would help Cody. She asked if any of us had any idea that Cody was in a mental health crisis. All of us sat there shaking our heads no. She then said she wasn't surprised; Cody was very good at hiding his feelings. She felt he was dealing with depression. Having talked with Cody, she felt encouraged that if he received proper medical and emotional treatment he could have a successful recovery. The word depression stirred up fear, but the word recovery spoke louder. That word spoke hope.

When she walked away, I thought about the word depression. That memory from the dinner table came flooding into the front of my brain. How did I not see this? He wasn't acting sad. He hadn't talked about being overwhelmed with school or schoolwork. I knew the current baseball season was tough, but never, never did I ever think he was in a mental health crisis. Depression and I became really close over the next eight months as I submerged myself into the world of mental health. I was determined to find out everything I could about this illness.

3

SEEING MY SON

It had been over two hours before Cody's nurse came out and said, "Cody is ready to see you. He would like to start with Dana, then Mom and Dad."

I didn't care that he didn't want to see us first. I trusted that Cody knew what he needed at that moment. I was just thrilled and relieved he was ready.

Dana got up and looked at us nervously. With as much confidence in my voice as I could muster, I said, "It's gonna be okay." She followed the nurse through the large ER doors. As they slowly closed behind her, I thought, *I don't even know what she's walking into. I couldn't prepare her.* This would be the beginning of my baby girl growing up too fast.

Time was moving so slow as we sat waiting for Dana. I couldn't focus on anything. My whole world was behind those doors and I had no idea what was happening. I was helpless. After what felt like a lifetime, those doors parted and I saw my girl walking toward us. Her eyes were red and swollen and her cheeks rosy. In the midst of tears, she smiled at her father and me. It was so beautiful. At that moment, I felt an unexplainable reaction of comfort release throughout my body. Her smile expressed hope. I stood up and hugged her.

"He's ready to see you and Dad," she said softly.

Will and I followed the nurse down the same path Dana had just come from. I felt anxious; my heart was racing. We walked to what looked like the back of the ER. I had slowed my pace to match the nurse's tempo. She wasn't moving fast enough for me. We approached what looked like a locked door. It said, "Hospital Personnel Only." The nurse had to use a special keycard that let us in. As we cleared that door, the next thing I noticed was a man. He had a kind face and was sitting outside in the hallway across from a door. Then I noticed what he was wearing.

He was a security guard placed outside Cody's door. *Oh my God, he is for Cody. What the hell is happening? Is this really what I am seeing?* The nurse led us into Cody's room. He was lying in a hospital bed wearing green scrub-type hospital clothes. I couldn't get past the nurse fast enough to wrap my arms round him. Cody just kept saying how sorry he was. Through my tears, I just kept repeating that it was okay, and it was going to be alright. I laid my head on his chest as I was hugging him. My racing heart began to subside. I felt his chest rising with each of his crying breaths. Every sound around me became muffled, except one. I could hear Cody's heart beating. It was rhythmic, soothing, and it said to me, *He's alive.* Only gratefulness filled my heart. This could have been so much worse.

Besides his apologies and our assurances that everything would be okay, there wasn't much else spoken between us. This first visit was about comforting him. We asked the nurse if she could have Dana come back. I wanted us all together.

Cody said he was struggling with a headache. When the nurse came back with Dana, we were able to get Cody some pain relief and let him rest. We all sat as close as we could to Cody as he rested. I didn't want to leave his side. I desperately wanted him to know he was going to be okay, even though I had no idea what that looked like. I didn't know how we'd gotten here. For sure, I didn't know where to go from here. I was focused on one thing: assuring Cody we were here no matter what the future held.

I was now in a world I didn't understand. I was going to need help. I was unprepared and afraid. What scared me most was failing my son, which was not an option. Each step from here was a step into the unknown. My son was in crisis and I didn't know the best way to help him. My daughter was in crisis and I didn't know the best way to help her, either.

When Cody woke, he said his headache was better and he wanted to talk.

"I'm ready to get help. I want to feel better," he said, still pale and hands slightly trembling. But there was strength behind his tired eyes, a strength that I knew so well.

"The social worker will be helping us," I said, making sure to include the family; I wanted him to understand he wasn't alone. "We all need help from her, and we're in this together with you."

I explained how the social worker had already started the process of determining a course of treatment. She had suggested a short-stay inpatient psychiatric treatment center. Cody was in agreement. We would work on finding him a bed opening tomorrow, as the two treatment centers were currently at capacity. It was close to midnight, and Cody was exhausted and needed sleep. I didn't want to leave, but no one was allowed to stay in his room overnight. We would be back first thing in the morning to begin what we thought would be a simple process of getting him a bed. This was the first of many processes we incorrectly assumed would be simple. Just the thought of him spending the night in the ER made me nauseous. But it was necessary. We gave Cody hugs and said our goodnights. At least I knew he wouldn't be alone. He would have someone sitting outside his door.

Will, Dana and I walked out of the hospital with family and friends. I asked my sister, Marita, if she was able to contact our brothers and sisters. We have a large family so that was not an easy task. I couldn't make all those calls and repeat the same conversation over and over; I trusted Marita to be my voice and convey exactly what was needed.

She said she got through to everyone except my oldest brother and his wife because they were on a cruise. My mother and another sister and her family were out of the country. Crises don't wait for everyone to be home.

Not only did Marita make those calls, but she started researching the process of getting Cody admitted into a treatment center. It wasn't until later that she shared how difficult it was for her to see me in such enormous pain that I was barely responsive. She said I hardly looked or acted like myself as she witnessed me in a state of absolute shock trying to emotionally grasp what was happening around me. Gratitude isn't a strong enough word to express how I felt about what she did for me and my family.

The one sibling I was eager to talk to was Gabe; he's closest in age to me, and we grew up side by side. He is my person. Our oldest brother Ev gave us the nickname "The Hoodlums". We went everywhere together. We protected each other in a home strained by an alcoholic father. We would often joke we were like twins; we knew each other's thoughts. There were no secrets between us, and we could trust each other to speak the truth when needed. The best part of our relationship is our laughter. I really missed him right now. I wanted to be the one to tell him about Cody, but I was too overwhelmed and I knew he would understand. I would call him in the morning.

During our drive home, my internal emotions were raging. I was screaming, crying, fear-ridden and angry. My guilt was building. I felt myself suffocating beneath it. I left a piece of my heart at that hospital. Another piece, Dana, was sitting in the back seat of the car and I didn't have the words to console her. She adores her brother. How was she coping? My fear for her was high, and my confidence as a mother was falling. How could I trust I would say the right thing?

Once home, I focused on getting Dana into bed. I tucked her in and said, "Cody is going to get the help he needs. He just isn't well right now. He's going to get better." I reassured her that he loved her. We hugged as I tucked her into bed. I had no idea if she was taking in anything I was saying.

I walked into my room on autopilot. I absentmindedly completed the mundane tasks of brushing my teeth, putting on my pajamas and feeding our dog. Looking back now, I can't say for sure if I did them, because I wasn't aware of what I was doing. Will was trying to comfort me, but I couldn't actually receive it. I was so lost. I was looking through a picture window at someone else's life – this couldn't be my life. I laid my head down on my pillow and begged for my mind to stop and for morning to come.

I know what you must be thinking – believe me, I thought it, too: "How did she miss that her son was suicidal? Why couldn't she tell he was in crisis? What's wrong with that mom?" At the time, it was easy to imagine those whispers would be passed between other moms and dads once more people knew about what happened.

Here's what I can tell you. I missed it because I wasn't equipped. What did I know? For us, it was important to talk to kids about drugs, alcohol, sex and pornography. We had had those conversations. I did my best to teach the kids about love, respect, good morals and work ethic. I taught them how to make their beds, do the dishes, and how to do a job well. But I didn't teach them about what happens when you wake up sad every morning, because I didn't have any tools for that kind of conversation. Or what to do when you feel unmotivated or have thoughts of suicide. It will be my most painful regret and lesson, and one that I didn't realize I needed. I was naive, uninformed, uneducated and wrong. Somewhere over the previous year, depression had sneaked in through my back door and almost took my son's life.

4

FROM A SHADY MOTEL
TO THE RITZ CARLTON

I woke from an extremely restless night's sleep. My thoughts immediately went to Cody and how quickly I could get to the hospital, but knew I needed to make two phone calls. I threw clothes on and immediately went downstairs. I would have a small window to talk to Gabe before Dana woke up. I gathered myself and dialed his number. The phone rang once before I heard him say my name. "Angie?" That's all it took, I just lost it and started crying.

He said to me, between my sobs, 'I'm on the first flight out of here today, I will be there late tonight around midnight."

I just continued to cry and tried to talk, and he let me do just that. No other words were necessary from him. He was on his way and that was all I needed to hear. After we hung up, I just sat on the floor and tried to calm myself. I had one more phone call to go: work. I called my co-worker and friend, Media. She was shocked and broke down with me on the phone. I knew she would take care of everything at work. I asked her not to talk to anyone about Cody until I had more details. We were a tight group at work, but I wasn't ready for that information to go out. It's unusual for me not to be at work, so I knew it was a big ask for her to keep it under wraps.

I could hear Dana and Will moving upstairs and knew they must be getting ready. We got out the door to be at the hospital by 8:30am. Not much was said in the car. We were all anxious to get to Cody and figure out the next steps to get him out of the ER, which wasn't the best environment. He was in the locked area of a ER, and everything in his room was either locked, out of the way or behind plexiglass – even the television was behind plexiglass. We knew we had to move him to somewhere better, but to where I didn't know.

Once we arrived at the ER, we went straight to Cody's room. A new security guard was at the same post as last night. Cody was sitting up in bed finishing breakfast. He looked up and smiled. He looked happy to see us and like he got some rest. He said his headache was better. After all our hugs, Cody asked that we not talk about what happened. He wanted help, but wanted to let that specific work start once he got in treatment. We all understood and accepted that, but it was still awkward at times because it was the "the elephant in the room", or more like a herd of elephants. We talked about what was happening in the world of sport, Dana's school, and sometimes we just sat and watched TV. It was about keeping the conversation light, only discussing his next steps to get into treatment.

We took turns sitting with Cody and then sitting in the waiting room with friends and family who came and went. I was working closely with the medical staff and my sister Marita who was employed at an area hospital. She was helping me work through everything necessary to get Cody fast-tracked for a bed – not an easy task. You would have thought that a suicide attempt was enough to warrant a transition to a hospital bed, but the system is flawed and overcrowded. It was a waiting game all day. As we waited, I was having to make decisions left and right. *Should Dana go to school tomorrow? Does Will need to ask for a leave of absence? Which treatment center looks better for Cody? Do I need to notify my insurance what was happening?* I was overwhelmed and felt inadequate in my ability to make even a simple decision. Someone asked me, "Do you want a ham or turkey sandwich?", and I just looked blankly at them – even that decision felt taxing.

When I was back with Cody, I got a text that the school district superintendent had arrived at the ER to show his support. I left Cody to go talk with him. I needed to figure out Cody and Dana's school situation. I knew the superintendent was there because he cared. The administration was doing a good job of keeping this private for our family. After talking with him I was relieved to hear that they had reviewed everything regarding Cody and Dana's schoolwork. Both of our children were doing well in school, and had met all the requirements for the year. So, if Cody didn't make it back this year, he would still be allowed to advance to the next grade, and the same went for Dana. That was a relief, and one less thing I had to think about. I was grateful.

Next decision. Someone asked me about Cody's car. I had almost forgotten about the car, but then realized it had been sitting at the location all night. This is where friends are your saving grace. There was no way that car was coming back to our house. I didn't ever want it back. Our friends not only went and got the car, but grabbed all of Cody's stuff from it and dropped it at our house. Then they stored the car for us. They knew we were not in a position right then to determine what to do with it. Much later on, they took it to another city and sold it for us. I didn't want to take the chance that any of us would see that car in our local area.

I went back to sit with Cody, and I could feel the heaviness of my eyes. It must have been in the air, because Cody said he needed to close his eyes and sleep for a little bit. I sat as close to him as I could and put my head next to his shoulder leaning on my arm against the rail. I kept dropping off and my head would hit the safety bar on the side; I was fighting to stay awake. All of a sudden, I felt the softness of a pillow getting tucked under my head. I lifted my heavy eyelids and saw our security guard slowly walking out of the room and sitting back in his seat. I smiled at him, and he smiled back. My eyes were grateful for rest. I was too tired to think what he must be thinking. For that moment his action of placing a pillow under my head gave me rest, not only in my mind but in my soul. I don't know how long we slept, but I knew he was watching out for us, and I was glad he was there.

By late afternoon we got the disappointing news that a bed wouldn't be available, but that Cody could be moved to Randall Children's Hospital to wait for a bed. He would be able to get out of the ER. I was in shock – I didn't even know that was an option. I was overjoyed. Cody had been to Randall when he was eight for a tethered cord spinal surgery. It was a beautiful hospital. We were not allowed to transport him there, so the hospital arranged a service to take him. I didn't even know about those types of services. As I was waiting in Cody's room, his nurse came in to tell us transport was on their way. She then began to talk to Cody gently, but with a serious tone.

She said, "Cody, when you get in treatment, work hard on getting better, because: one, you're 17. You don't want to be back here as an adult. Things change. Your mom would not be able to be back here with you, helping you through this process. And two, getting a transitional bed at Randall doesn't happen while you're waiting to go into inpatient treatment. Some patients wait up to a week in the ER before a bed opens up. This is a mini miracle, so you go make the best of it."

I saw on Cody's face that he was taking in every word she said. Cody looked at her straight in the eye and said he would, he said he wanted to feel better. I sat in awe, knowing her words were another gift to us along with all my sister Marita was doing. Transport arrived, I had to say goodbye to Cody in his room. The nurse said she would get him ready and that we could see Cody leave from the ambulance bay.

I hugged Cody and said, "I'll see you at Randalls." He looked nervous.

I walked out to the waiting room and we watched as a dark sedan marked with the word "Transport" drove in. It was only maybe five minutes before we saw them leave. A woman was in the passenger side and a man was driving. As sad as it looked with Cody sitting alone in the right backseat, I knew this meant treatment was one step closer. It took me a while before I didn't see the "Transport" on every sedan in traffic and not think of that ride Cody took alone.

By the time Will, Dana and I arrived at Randall Children's Hospital and checked in, we were told Cody was already in his room on the third floor. We headed up in the elevator and, as we walked down the hall, we saw what looked like a nurse sitting outside a door. I gathered that must be Cody's room. I found out that the person sitting outside his door was called a sitter; there would be someone there until he went to treatment. I understood why, but it still felt awkward.

I walked into his room and was instantly relieved. His room was large and beautifully furnished for a hospital room. Cody's bed was in the middle and on his right was a picture window overlooking the grounds, with a long padded bench seat. A rocking chair sat in one corner and there was more seating throughout the room. There was no stale hospital smell, no plexiglass covering the TV, nothing was locked up, and he even had his own bathroom. What a change from where he had been. We went from a dark, shady motel to the Ritz Carlton. Cody was sitting up in his bed watching TV. We had brought him fresh clothes, toiletries and his computer. He was grateful to do something else besides watch television or try to make conversation. Will, Dana and I sat on the window seat. We hadn't been there very long before a doctor arrived to do a check-up, but not your normal check-up. Some of the questions were basic, but I knew the doctor was evaluating Cody's mental state and making an assessment.

My fatigue, from restless sleep and adrenaline overload, was overtaking me. I allowed myself to stretch out on the window bench to lay my head on Will's lap and my feet on Dana's legs. I could hear the TV going and Cody's fingers on the keyboard; at this moment my family was together and safe. I couldn't keep my eyes open any longer, sleep couldn't wait any longer. The sitter outside Cody's door must have seen me, and came into the room without me even hearing her and draped a warm blanket over me. It was all I needed. I drifted off to a peaceful sleep thinking of how kind she was.

I woke up and, judging by the fading light outside, it was getting late. Dana planned on going to school the next day. They were presenting the Student of the Month Award and she was nominated. I knew she was the winner. They let the parents know first so we can be in the audience. She wanted to be there in case she did receive it, and it would have been strange if she wasn't. I thought about the baseball game that Cody was supposed to be playing in. I knew players were wondering where Cody was. Jenni, the mom I had called on the way to the ER, had texted me earlier that a number of parents and players were asking where Cody was. At this point, only the coaches and Mitchell knew what had happened. I couldn't think about that next step yet. I understood why Dana felt the need to go to school; she deserved and had earned that award. She needed some type of normal, even if it was only for a couple of hours.

Gabe texted me to confirm his flight was on time to arrive close to 11:30pm. He would need to rent a car, so he said to expect him at our house by 12:15am. Will and I agreed that Will would stay the night with Cody at the hospital and I would head home with Dana. I couldn't wait to see Gabe, not only for me, but for Dana. It would be good to have him at home when I needed to be with Cody.

5

MY DAUGHTER

I was anxious during the drive home, but I couldn't pinpoint exactly what was causing it, which made it hard to calm myself. I just knew fear was surfacing and could feel my skin crawling. Maybe it was the quietness of the drive giving me too much time to think, or when I looked at Dana in the passenger seat and wished I could read her mind and know how she was really doing. I turned on the radio; we both needed the distraction.

Dana and I arrived home exhausted. I made sure to leave the back sliding door open for Gabe. I asked Dana if she would sleep with me that night. We both needed each other and I hated the idea of being separated. It was comforting knowing she was next to me.

We laid our heads down and I tried to sleep. Tears were rolling down my face and I was trying to get my thoughts to stop the what-ifs. But they were running away with me. What if the cyclist hadn't found Cody? What if he tries this again? What if I miss it again? My mind began to relive the last 36 hours. I'd heard somewhere that during a crisis you can lose blocks of time and memories – I believe it; it was happening to me. I wasn't able to recall everything. There were too many interactions and conversations to count. Thank God for my sister and close friends; they fielded and screened so many calls for me. I knew my family wanted to hear my voice, but I just couldn't talk yet. I was so tired. It felt as if I had lived a lifetime during each day since this happened. I whispered to myself, *Go to sleep Angie, hold onto hope.*

I must have fallen asleep because I was jolted awake by the sound of someone trying to be quiet coming up the stairs. *Gabe's here*, I thought. I walked out of my bedroom and hugged him. We didn't say much, just enough to let him know the plan for tomorrow. I would go to Dana's school assembly, and then leave Gabe with Dana as I headed down to Randalls. My other brother Mark was arriving tomorrow and Gabe was planning to pick him up, and he let me know they would come to the hospital after he arrived. I thanked him for coming and we both went to bed, it was late.

I woke before Dana and quietly got dressed; I needed some coffee. As I left my bedroom, I noticed that Gabe's door was open and his bed empty. I met him downstairs, and as I made coffee we kept the conversation light. Dana was upstairs and I didn't want her to overhear anything she shouldn't. I reaffirmed the plan for the day, since we were both half asleep last night and I didn't trust that I told him everything he needed. I went and woke Dana to get ready for school. I whispered that her Uncle Gabe was there and she smiled. It would be a tough day for her, but having her uncle there would make it bearable.

I remember dropping Dana off at school that morning. I would be back shortly for the assembly, but watching her courageously walk into the school alone was painful. She promised she'd call if she wasn't doing well so that Gabe or I could come and get her. Knowing that her principal and school counselor were aware of the situation made it easier for me to let her go to school, but it didn't change the fact that Dana would be putting on a brave front to get through her day.

Once back home, I sat with Gabe and talked without a filter. Having him there made me calmer. I knew his presence would give Dana reassurance that it's all going to be okay. I trusted him with her emotions, I knew he would be just what she needed while Will and I needed to be with Cody. I left him with my scribbled notes of instructions and headed to the assembly.

Dana's principal greeted me as I walked in – she must have been watching out for me. She gave me a hug and then took a few minutes to talk with me about Dana and how they could provide support as we walked to the gymnasium. I thanked her and said I'd be in touch if we needed something, but at this point, we weren't sure. The top of the bleachers had the best view so I headed there to sit. Dana didn't know I would be there because although she knew she was nominated for Student of the Month, you don't know if you win until the assembly itself, so I wasn't worried about her seeing me. The kids were walking in and I chuckled at the sight of the teachers as they tried to corral all the kids to take their seats for the award presentation.

The sixth and seventh graders' awards were first; then it was time for Dana. I could see a group of her friends gathering together and heading to the podium. They took turns saying why they nominated Dana for Student of the Month, then they called her name and she walked up to receive her award. Those friends didn't know the amount of pain she was in. What a strange and lonely experience it must have been for her. I wanted to take her pain away. Dana found me in the crowd and we made eye contact – it was as if all time had stopped. It was just me and Dana at that moment and we smiled at each other. I could see the sadness in her eyes; she was going through the motions as she took her seat. The ache in my heart for her was heavy.

Dana had lovely teachers and support staff who I knew would take extra care to make sure she was doing okay. They didn't know all the details but knew there was a family situation. Dana asked that I not say anything to her teachers about Cody until she felt ready, or she decided to tell them herself. I understood. I was hopeful that being at school would provide her some sort of normal – she needed that. I hugged her goodbye and reminded her that Uncle Gabe was excited to pick her up from school and hang out. I could tell by her face that she was glad of that too.

6

LITTLE CLUES

I headed home and went into Cody's room to grab him clothes in preparation for what the day could hold. I noticed the hospital bag on his floor with the clothes that he wore the night he was admitted into the ER. They had changed him into scrubs once he arrived and put his clothes in this bag. They gave me the bag after he was checked out of the ER on his way to Randall Children's Hospital, and I totally forgot about them. I sat on his bed and opened the bag. There, all crumpled, was the baseball uniform he had on the night they found him. I sat holding them with waves of thankful emotions rushing over me. I didn't want to leave them in the bag, so I decided to start a small load of laundry before I left. I went through his pockets to get out the little pieces of dirt that get in there and found something in his back pocket. I pulled out a receipt. I quickly scanned it, not thinking anything in particular until I noticed what was purchased. My hands started to shake. The receipt was dated May 1st and the time stamp was from after his baseball game that night; it was for the items that Cody used to attempt suicide. I slid down the wall in the laundry room, grabbed my knees and began the painful sobs of acknowledgement that I had found another piece of this painful puzzle. Why, why was this happening to Cody? I don't know how long I sat there. I felt a vibration in my pocket that brought me back to the present. It was Cody's phone which I had picked up and put in my pocket earlier. He was starting to receive new text messages. *I can't handle that right now*, I said to myself, *I know the team and friends are wondering where he is, but I just can't deal with it.* I stood up, pulled myself together and headed to the hospital.

When I arrived, Cody seemed well, but I didn't believe anything I saw. I had lost my ability to trust him, or even myself. Because we had agreed not to discuss the situation, I started off by sharing what was happening with my upcoming race. Over the previous couple of years, I had been putting on a race called "Run Girlfriend Run". It was a 5k/10k run to raise money for the scholarships that I provided to middle and high school girls to help with school, club sports and activities. It was in a couple of weeks and I honestly didn't know how I was going to manage it – I just didn't feel like I had it in me. Cody must have been reading my face because he told me I couldn't miss being at my race. I knew it too, because there was no way I was going to have him feel bad, and there was no way Dana was not going to have something to look forward to – but my heart was just not there. The idea of going to work, let alone putting a race on, was not even in my thought process as a priority. My mind was filtering out what it didn't think was critical. I was fortunate that my co-worker Media knew everything about the race and was working through the last-minute details. Plus, our close friends and family were my course markers and volunteer organizers; they would hold me up during those final two weeks of race prep.

There were numerous check-in visits with doctors throughout the day as we waited for a bed. One nurse shared that the inpatient treatment center building was right next to us. As the day progressed, Will and I both started receiving phone messages and texts from people asking about Cody, trying to confirm things they heard. We didn't know how information was getting out, but we needed a plan. I didn't reply to any messages until I got one that made me hold my breath; I tried to remain calm so no one could read my face.

It was from a close friend and it read, "Angie, I heard what happened with Cody and I just want you to know we are thinking about you. I believe I know who saved Cody that night." I nonchalantly let Will read the text. His eyes got big. I made some excuse that I needed to stretch my legs and went for a walk. I found a private spot at the end of the corridor and sat on the floor to call her. So many questions went through my mind. *How did she hear about Cody? How did she know who saved him? I didn't even know that.* I dialed her number and within seconds she answered. She didn't know what to say to me, except she'd been praying for us.

I replied quickly, "Thank you, but how do you know what happened, and who saved Cody?"

I'm sure I sounded impatient but I was so desperate for any piece of information. She said a friend of hers heard the story directly from him.

I asked again, "Who is he?"

"His name is Brock, but I don't know his last name, but he lives somewhere in Boring," she said.

"What? In Boring!" I said, "Where?"

All I could think was how crazy it was that he lived in our same town. *What is happening?* She mentioned a street name that I didn't recognize completely. It sounded close to the name of a road I knew, but she couldn't confirm. I asked her if she could get more information and to keep our conversation private.

I hung up the phone and could feel tears wanting to come. *Not now Angie, you have to wait,* I thought. I wanted so much to lie on the floor and sob. I texted Will what had happened and took a few minutes to compose myself before I went back to Cody's room.

It wasn't long before Gabe arrived with Dana. I met them in the waiting room and sent Dana to be with Cody as I stayed with Gabe. Marita and my niece Courtney arrived not long after; they knew they couldn't see Cody, but they wanted to bring me some food, and say hello to Gabe. I left the three of them in the waiting room and headed back to Cody.

The news arrived that an inpatient bed would be ready around 6pm that evening. We were excited and relieved. Randall Children's Hospital had been wonderful, but we were all ready for Cody to start to get the help he needed. We'd decided that Dana wasn't to be part of Cody's transition into treatment as there were too many unknowns. The nurse came in to make sure we were packed up and let us know it should be anytime. Dana said her goodbyes and I walked her out to Gabe and my other brother Mark, who greeted her with smiles and hugs. I let her know I'd call right after we got Cody in his room so she would know her brother was okay. I gave her a hug and headed back to Cody's room.

The nurse was wrapping up Cody's transfer paperwork, and from the window she pointed out the treatment center. It was an older building with an attached courtyard. Will and I looked out and saw the beautiful courtyard with a basketball hoop, but we didn't see anyone outside. I tried to envision our son there, maybe sitting in the courtyard or shooting baskets. I was glad he would have a nice outside space. There were different treatment centers in Portland, but I had gone with the recommendations my sister Marita had received, and trusted this was the right move. The nurse finished up and we waited. My nerves were raw and my stomach was doing flips. I couldn't imagine how Cody felt. We focused on positive conversation, watched some TV and celebrated that Cody was able to shower and get changed into real clothes. It was such a strange experience to be in a hospital room knowing that physically Cody was fine, but what was happening inside his brain wasn't fine. Now hope was coming.

7

THE LONG HALLWAY TO HELP

A new nurse arrived with a wheelchair and said it was time to go. I was surprised Cody wasn't allowed to walk, but in the time it took me to think that thought the explanation arrived in the form of a security guard who came up beside the nurse and introduced himself. I don't remember his name. I was irritated; I understood, but I didn't like it, and I didn't like being surprised by it. I wished they would have mentioned that security personnel would be escorting us to treatment. My irritation changed immediately to concern when I looked down at Cody in that wheelchair – he was physically shaking.

He looked at me and whispered, "Mom, I'm scared." My heart caved in.

I looked at his face, took hold of his shaking hand and said with as much calmness and strength that I could, "Me too, but we are going to be here for you every day, and this is where help is. It's going to be okay. You can do this."

I wanted to grab him in my arms and take his pain away from him. I felt helpless and kept questioning in my mind whether we were doing the right thing. Then, I thought of all the mini miracles that got us to this point and I believed in the importance of this moment for all of us.

We went down in an elevator in silence, and after a number of turns started down a long hallway. It seemed to take forever to reach a set of double doors. I can't remember how we actually got there, nor could I have retraced my steps. We passed through the doors and ended up in a conference room. The nurse and the security guard said our intake nurse would be with us shortly and left us. Cody was still shaking. I tried to stay as positive as I could. I couldn't imagine how this would be if Cody was not receptive to getting help. This room didn't send off any inviting or peaceful vibes – it seemed scary.

The intake nurse came in and, honestly, it was not a great first impression. She didn't make eye contact and seemed rushed and preoccupied. My fear and anger were rising. I thought to myself, *How can I leave my son here with this person?* but I also knew I wasn't capable of giving him the help he needed. I wanted to shake that nurse and tell her to pull herself together. I needed her to be on her A game. The conflict in me was overwhelming, but I needed Cody to see nothing but strength and security in me. I pulled from everything I had to put my best face on.

The nurse sat down, introduced herself and began to explain what to expect during treatment. Cody was to be at the center for between five and eight days as it was a short-term inpatient treatment center. They wouldn't know until Cody was evaluated if a longer program was needed. We were told we could visit him every day and call him twice a day during visiting hours. I asked if Dana could come. She nodded yes, and said family involvement was a critical part of treatment and recovery. I breathed easier knowing we could see Cody every day; I saw relief on Cody's face too. The nurse's personality was becoming warmer as she continued to speak, and my anger started to subside. Cody would have a bedroom to himself, but needed to know he would be on video, except in the bathroom.

She then gave us a tour of the center. It was strange for me to imagine Cody living here for the next week or so. I looked at Cody and wondered how he was doing. She showed us the kitchen and group therapy and activity areas. On our way to Cody's room, she showed us where we would check in during our visits and introduced us to one of the main desk employees responsible for monitoring the center's security cameras.

Next was Cody's bedroom. We walked round a corner and down a hall with a number of doors. She pulled out her keys and unlocked one. She said to head in and get settled and she would be back soon to have Will and me sign some paperwork.

The room looked like a college dorm room. The floor was old white hospital vinyl squares. It had a bed, desk, sink, closet and an attached private bathroom. I was glad he had a large picture window that overlooked the courtyard. I noticed the cameras in the corner. It was all so surreal.

I handed Cody the bag I had packed for him earlier in the day. The center had given me a list of items and clothing he would need for his stay, while also outlining what wasn't allowed. For example, he would need a sweatshirt, but it couldn't have a drawstring. He would need shoes, but they couldn't have laces. They suggested slide sandals for showers and walking around. He couldn't have a cellphone, but could have books, paper, pens and pencils. Pictures were encouraged as long as they were not in a glass frame. Music was allowed, but it needed to be a radio, not an iPod. He could have a toothbrush and toothpaste, but no razors. It was not your normal list of items for going on a trip.

I had picked clothes for Cody that were soft and comfortable. I had removed the shoelaces from his tennis shoes and the drawstrings from his sweatshirts and sweatpants. I had brought pictures of us and our dog, Cocoa, along with paper and pen. Cody was grateful to be surrounded by his own stuff. He thought of a few other things he would like, which included a radio and certain books. I made a list of things and promised I'd bring them during our visit the following day.

The nurse came back in and it was time for Will and me to sign papers and say goodnight. She set up a time for us to meet Cody's doctors and the social worker who would be managing his care and going over his treatment plan. I didn't want to leave him, but I had to be careful of my reactions. I wanted him to feel safe and good about the fact that he was going to get help. Will and I said goodnight, gave hugs and a strong, *I love you, you've got this*. I knew we would see him in the morning which made it easier to walk out the door.

The nurse escorted us out and walked us through the protocol for future visits. There would be two security areas to pass through and we would be unable to bring anything except items necessary for the visit. We could bring Cody outside food, clean clothes and other approved items, but no purses, wallets or cellphones. There would be lockers after the first security area where we could put our belongings before entering the actual center.

I was taking in all the information and could only think *WOW*. She walked us to the exit and nodded to the staff in the camera room to unlock the door for us to leave. We thanked her as we left. I noticed, as the door was closing behind me, a sign on the front that said, "Watch for Runners." It took me until the next day to understand what that meant.

As we walked toward the exit door, I noticed a set of double security doors on the left. It said, "Adult Psychiatric Treatment Center" I could see inside and noticed older looking men walking around. I remembered back to what our ER nurse told us before we were transported. I was so grateful Cody was 17 and therefore still a minor and in a treatment center with patients his age.

Once at the exit door, we were instructed to push the button and the staff in the camera room would buzz us through. We went through the second security door and into the room with lockers and an elevator. I heard the door lock behind us. With that sound, everything became real.

I had just left my son somewhere with people I didn't know. I didn't know how he was going to be treated. I didn't trust the system, because I didn't know the system. I was told this was a good place for Cody, that he would be getting the help he needed. I wasn't convinced. Where were the parent reviews showing me a rating scale of care; great nurses, wonderful doctors, incredible programs, great success rate of recovery? I wanted a five-star treatment center.

Will and I had only said a few words since we had left Cody's room. One of us must have pushed the elevator button, because all of a sudden the door opened. Will and I stepped in and pushed the down button. As the door closed, Will leaned against the back elevator wall and began to sob. Tears also began streaming down my face as I lay my head on his shoulder; neither one of us could say a thing. I held onto the rails in that elevator as if I was holding on for my life. I wanted this ride to stop. We got in our car and I called Dana right away to let her know her brother was in the treatment center and doing okay. She was excited that she would be able to visit him tomorrow. I promised to fill her in more when we got home, but assured her he was on his way to recovery.

I couldn't wait to see and hug Dana. I was pleased to hear she had had a good day with her uncles and Courtney. I explained that she would visit Cody the following afternoon because her dad and I had appointments in the morning with Cody's doctors and social worker. She understood; she was just excited she could visit.

Tomorrow would be another big day and my body needed to rest and I needed to get some sleep. I chose to only focus on positive facts as I lay there. *Cody was getting the help he needed, he was in a safe place, a camera was watching him 24 hours a day and someone was there all night making sure he was safe.* It gave me peace to sleep.

8

THE DIAGNOSIS – DEPRESSION

I thought, "I'm a man – I can't talk about how I feel or share
this with anyone." And so I shoved it away.
Cody Welty

Early morning came and I had slept better. My head was
clearer. Our appointment was not scheduled for a couple of
hours, which gave me time to address how to communicate
what had happened to Cody to the outside world. We were
discovering that the information out there in the community
was wrong. Our friends and family were getting phone calls,
and they didn't want to confirm or deny anything so they just
told all who asked that they were not able to discuss anything.
We didn't want rumors flying around, especially since Dana
wanted to finish out the school year. We heard students from
their schools were distraught and struggling because of the
rumors, and were trying to reach out to Cody. We had talked
to Cody during his stay at Randalls and he had agreed that
some type of information needed to be communicated. He
trusted us with what to say, and had asked that we start with
the baseball and softball teams first. I was able to make a
phone call to Wade that same day and let him know I would
formulate a letter he could read or hand out to the teams during
the upcoming mandatory fundraiser flower pick up meeting.
Parents and coaches would be there during the meeting and

so could provide much-needed support to their child(ren). We were all trying to make the best decisions as issues arose. This school and community had no experience of handling this type of communication.

This sounded good in theory, but I was severely struggling with writing that letter. I tried several times, only to get agitated. Gabe made an excellent suggestion after hearing me crumple up a third piece of paper. He thought I should call Tori, my niece. As Tori was a teacher for another school district, he thought she may have a better handle on what parents needed to hear. Best advice ever. Gabe was able to get me started and then we turned it over to Tori. What she put together was perfect. I emailed the document to the Athletic Director and Wade, and they took it from there. That letter ended up being used as an excellent communication tool for all of Cody's and Dana's teachers and coaches; I even used it for my work staff. The gym where I worked was a second home to my children and to so many of the students and parents in our community. This wasn't a situation that was going to stay quiet, so we were trying our best to minimize any impact on Cody and Dana and to stop any rumors by getting the facts out. I was so glad and relieved it was done.

Will and I headed to our appointment with Cody's treatment team. Dana stayed back with my brothers until she could visit later in the afternoon. It was a 45-minute drive, with an additional 10 minutes to get checked in through security. We were shown to a conference room with a large round table for the meeting. Cody's social worker was first to arrive; he introduced himself and said we would be meeting with him first and then the team of doctors would come in. I liked him; he had a calm demeanor and friendly smile – very easy-going. He said he had met with Cody already and felt they had had a great first meeting. He explained his role as Cody's social worker: he would be helping him and us work through this crisis and develop a course of action. That sounded wonderful to me. Finally! I was getting some good, solid information.

He went on to explain in great detail that Cody had been diagnosed with depression and that the doctors had already placed him on a low-dose antidepressant in conjunction with cognitive therapy.

Cognitive behavioral therapy (CBT) is a form of psychotherapy that focuses on modifying dysfunctional emotions, behaviors, and thoughts by interrogating and uprooting negative or irrational beliefs. Considered a "solutions-oriented" form of talk therapy, CBT rests on the idea that thoughts and perceptions influence behavior.[1]

The social worker shared Cody's daily schedule of a typical day. It included private and group counseling sessions, education classes and free time and meal schedules. He reiterated the importance of family connection. They encouraged a daily visit, with a morning and evening phone call. My hope bucket was filling up. I was gaining knowledge and education. The diagnosis of depression didn't feel as scary or heavy. My son was getting the treatment and tools he needed to start his road to recovery, and so were we. It was encouraging to be around professionals who had the experience to help our family through this crisis. I wasn't being naive – I realized we were still in the infancy of this diagnosis, but we had a plan, we had hope and we were not letting go of that.

Cody's doctors arrived just as we were wrapping up with his social worker. There were two doctors, a man and a woman. The first thing I noticed was their positivity balanced with seriousness. They too had met with Cody and they shared how his openness to getting help would be a strong component for his path to recovery. He had already attended one group session and class and was responding well. They explained that he would continue to learn and understand his depression

1   Cited from www.psychologytoday.com/gb/basics/cognitive-behavioral-therapy.

diagnosis through the classes. He would learn about personal triggers, coping skills and techniques, and what his medication does. I did have questions about the medication; I wanted to understand in more detail its value and what the side effects were. They had chosen Celexa, the generic form is called citalopram. They said there may be a few side effects; however, they should be minimal, and he would be monitored.

Citalopram is in the class of drugs called selective serotonin reuptake inhibitors (SSRIs). Citalopram is used to treat depression. It may improve your energy level and feelings of well-being. This medication works by helping to restore balance of a certain natural substance (serotonin) in the brain.[2]

At night he was to be given melatonin to help with restless sleep. He had a hard time staying asleep.

Melatonin's main job in the body is to regulate night and day cycles or sleep-wake cycles. Darkness causes the body to produce more melatonin, which signals the body to prepare for sleep. Light decreases melatonin production and signals the body to prepare for being awake. Some people who have trouble sleeping have low levels of melatonin. It is thought that adding melatonin from supplements might help them sleep.[3]

I learned how important sleep is when treating depression.

The relationship between sleep and mood is complex, because disrupted sleep can lead to emotional changes, clinical depression or anxiety (as well as other psychiatric

2 Cited from www.webmd.com/drugs/2/drug-1701/citalopram-oral/details.

3 Cited from www.webmd.com/vitamins/ai/ingredientmono-940/melatonin.

conditions), but these conditions can also compound or further disrupt sleep. In fact, altered sleep patterns are a hallmark of many mental health issues. [4]

Each piece of new information I received replaced the buckets of fear with hope. It's not that it wasn't scary to hear and learn about Cody's diagnosis – because it was – but treatment was available. It felt good to be sitting with Cody's team of mental health professionals, knowing they were there to help Cody and our family through this. It gave me the courage I needed.

We were informed about a parent class that was mandatory before Cody would be allowed to come home. It was scheduled for the Tuesday night of the following week. It was going to give us more knowledge and understanding about what Cody was experiencing in his depression, and how better to support him. We would be meeting other parents whose children were also in treatment with Cody. I looked forward to anything that gave me the education and tools to help maneuver through this journey. I wanted to look into someone else's eyes who was going through something similar.

After our meeting we got to briefly see Cody. He looked alright. He shared that getting to sleep on the first night was rough, but then he said he told himself this, "This is my home for right now and I will make the best of it." I told him he was brave and he was going to get through this. I was overwhelmed with compassion for him.

I reminded Cody that the letter was going to be read tomorrow morning and that I might be getting more text messages to his phone. I needed clarification on how he would want me to respond. He thought for a minute, then said anyone who wanted to reach out to him could via a letter that we could bring to him on our visits. Then he could respond to each one

4   Cited from Jennifer Hines, "The Complex Relationship Between Sleep, Depression & Anxiety", Alaska Sleep Education Center, 29 May 2020.

personally. I thought that was brilliant. We agreed that after the teams were notified, Wade could use that letter as needed and that the same message about the letters could go to anyone who asked. I planned to call Wade later and let him know the new plan. I had a feeling the word would spread faster than we expected once the announcement was made, since text messaging and social media were how our young people communicated. We wrapped up our visit and said we would be back later with Dana. As I was leaving, I asked if he wanted us to bring anything back for him.

He said smiling softly, "Maybe a Jamba juice?"

"We can do that," I said with a smile.

Once we got home, I found Dana and Gabe watching *Pitch Perfect*. On any other day that would have seemed just a normal part of a visit from Uncle Gabe. We are a big movie family, so sitting around watching movies is one of our things. But this picture looked different to me – my brother was here for another reason I still hadn't wrapped my head around.

Before heading back to see Cody, I received a call from Wade who was thrilled with the letter idea. Many of Cody's close friends were struggling, and just knowing Cody would read their letter felt like a connection for them. I asked Wade to call me after the announcement; I wanted to be prepared for any phone calls or text messages.

Dana was beyond excited to see Cody. We explained during the drive what to expect, and that it looked worse than it was. That was the truth. We stopped and got him and Dana both a Jamba juice – I wasn't going to forget that request! Check-in went smoothly, and our first full family visit was under way. Cody hugged Dana first, and we all found a seat in his bedroom. He was very excited for the Jamba juice, some outside food.

A new doctor came in and checked on Cody and introduced himself. He started right off by saying to Will and me, "Well, if I could have gotten to Cody about six months ago, we would have been able to get on top of his depression."

I stared back at him as I was screaming at him in my mind, *Are you kidding me? Why did you just tell me that? I can't go back in time. Don't you think I'd want to go back in time?!* I was crushed. I somehow put it somewhere in my brain, but obviously not far enough back, because that comment haunted me for a long time.

"Oh, okay," was all I could reply. Luckily, only Will and I heard his comment because Cody and Dana were on the bed laughing.

I refocused on Cody and Dana and how happy they were to see each other. Cody began to tell us about his day and a funny mishap about forgetting his towel for the shower and having to run out naked to grab it knowing the cameras were on him. We got a good laugh at that one. He shared with us a packet of information explaining depression, and was visibly excited about what he was learning. He said he didn't feel alone, and that there was a reason he felt the way he did. He was getting help and the answers he so desperately needed. I held on to his every word. I saw relief, a sparkle in his eyes. He talked with hope and joy in his voice. It was a new day, a new sunrise.

Even though we didn't want to leave him, and he didn't want us to go, we all knew we would see him tomorrow, which helped. We said our goodbyes and had, for the first time, a pleasant drive home. We walked into our house and smelt the fresh scent of cleaning products. I looked up the stairs to see one brother vacuuming stairs and the other cleaning the kids' bathroom. They didn't hear us come in, so when I hollered "hello" we scared both of them silly. It was a very thoughtful thing for them to do, as cleaning my house was not a priority for me.

I tried for an hour to get to sleep that night, but failed. I walked downstairs and turned on the computer and started down the dark path of internet information on depression and treatment. Even though just hours before I had felt secure and courageous, fear was creeping back in. I was getting lost in depression and suicide medical terminology and drug side effects, and nothing I was reading made me feel hopeful. I needed some real-life stories. I finally shut my computer down and decided to wait until the class next week and talk to the professionals. The vastness of the internet wasn't helping me – I needed to start small.

I crawled between my sheets and thought about what tomorrow held. The letter would be read to the teams, which meant the privacy for Cody and our family I was holding on to would be gone. I trusted there was a reason for all of this and knew the information needed to be out there, but the formality of that letter made it that much more real. If Cody and all of us were going to heal, then the truth needed to be told. I hoped this would save Dana from whispers in the school hallway. While Cody was in the treatment world focusing on his recovery path, Dana was walking on a new path herself. This was our new reality, and I wasn't giving up on hope.

10

THE CYCLIST

My phone rang and I could see it was my girlfriend, Jenni. Before I could get out a hello, she said, "You are never going to believe this?" At this point, I had lost my ability to be surprised about anything.

"What is going on?" I asked hesitantly.

"The cyclist who saved Cody is our neighbor," she said elated. "He's our neighbor," she repeated, overjoyed.

"What?!" I said loudly. I hadn't meant to react that way.

I had to mouth "Everything's okay" to Will and Dana as I exited the room and raced up the stairs to my bedroom for privacy. I was eager to hear her story.

I had been wondering where the cyclist lived ever since I got that text from my other girlfriend. She knew his first name and mentioned a street name she thought he lived on, but even though he lived in my town, I couldn't find the actual street.

I was extremely excited to find out what Jenni knew. I sat down in my rocking chair and said, "Okay. I'm ready. Tell me the story."

"Angie, I can't believe it, but he is our next-door neighbor," she said through tears.

"Wait, you're telling me, he lives next door to you?" I was shaking my head in disbelief.

"Exactly," she said.

"Tell me the whole story. You have to start from the beginning, I need every detail," I said impatiently. I was glued to her every word.

She said she found out his identity by accident. She was doing yard work when her son Mitchell pulled into their driveway on his return from the fundraiser flower pick up meeting. Mitchell had left before Wade shared the letter with everyone, since he already knew everything about Cody.

As Mitchell got out of his car, he noticed their neighbor, Brock, walking toward him. Once he reached Mitchell, he asked him how Cody was doing. Mitchell paused and looked at Jenni, who had overheard the question and stopped what she was doing. They were both taken aback as to why their neighbor would be asking about Cody. She knew Mitchell would be unsure how to answer that seemingly simple question and quickly walked over to help him. She gently asked Brock why he was asking about Cody. He explained that he knew Mitchell played on the Sandy High School baseball team, so he had assumed he played with Cody. He then told them what Jenni couldn't fathom, that he was the one who found Cody that night in his car and rescued him. He further explained that Cody was wearing a Sandy Pioneers baseball uniform the night he found him and assumed Mitchell knew what had happened. Jenni couldn't contain herself – she threw her arms around him and thanked him for saving Cody and began to cry. She couldn't believe what she had heard. They spent the next 30 minutes sharing and updating him on Cody. She also told him I was looking forward to talking to him, and asked him if it was okay for her to give me his contact information. He said yes, and she said she couldn't get in the house fast enough to call me.

I sat there trying to analyze all the information Jenni had shared. I started crying on the phone – but these were good tears: tears of joy, tears of happiness. She was crying too, and we gave ourselves a minute. Time flew as we talked and talked about the experience. We were both amazed. Over an hour had passed; it was getting late and we were both talked out. Before we hung up, I grabbed a piece of paper and wrote down his name and cellphone number. I sat there looking at the name and number, knowing I had the ability right now to call him and get my final puzzle piece of that night, but I wasn't ready. That call would take more strength than I had at that moment. I put the piece of paper somewhere safe. I knew the family was wondering what the phone call was about and I couldn't wait to share the story. What are the odds that the man who saves your son's life lives in the same town, next to one of your son's best friends? I walked downstairs and into the family room where they all stopped what they were doing and stared at me. All I said was, "I found the cyclist who saved Cody."

Their faces, I'm sure, looked like mine when Jenni first told me. We finally knew who our hero was. Now, what do I do with the information?

11

THE LETTERS

That one letter that Wade shared with the teams and parents started a chain reaction of letters to Cody. They were coming from both his close friends and students he didn't know, and from freshmen to seniors, and even from students from other schools who knew him; from coaches, teachers, administrators, other parents; from family and close friends. So many letters.

The most amazing part is that because Cody didn't have access to his phone, the majority of all this communication was handwritten. Only a few were emails or text messages sent through me. Even though these letters were private to Cody, he did share a few with me. They were beautiful. You could see each personality within the handwritten words, and some even used artwork to communicate – things you can't always pick up in a text or an email. There was acceptance, compassion and humor. There was understanding, gratitude and love. The letters were one of the most beautiful expressions of loving someone I had seen. I felt privileged, in those few letters Cody did share, to see the depths of their souls, their vulnerability, and how openly they shared with Cody. Each one of those letters played a role in Cody's recovery.

We ended up having to bring more paper and pens to Cody. He had committed himself to writing back to everyone who wrote him a letter. Even after treatment was over, the letters kept coming, and Cody kept responding. Cody would tell you that it helped him heal; writing was an active tool of learning how to share his emotions, how to share pain, and that he was not alone. As much as they were showing love to Cody, he was reciprocating that love.

Our family also received an outpouring of cards sent to us from kids, teachers, friends and their families.

What I didn't realize until years later was that as Wade was receiving those letters to deliver to us, he was also involved in a major mental health awakening. Wade shared what it was like for him being at the school during that time. These are his actual words:

> The news of Cody's attempted suicide was not something that his classmates wanted. This was clear in every conversation I had with students. It was shocking. They all looked up to Cody, more than he ever realized. However, they did need something to make them feel like it was ok that they were going through some of the same things. They had similar doubts, fears, anxieties. Things that they could not articulate. Partially because there was an underlying fear of the shame that it would bring just by saying it out loud. Partially because they could not understand the feelings themselves. Sort of like not being able to ask a question about something you don't understand because you can't make enough sense of it to even be able to articulate the question. I can't tell you how many conversations had the same theme running through it. These kids were part of the cultural mainstream, coming from loving, middle class families and living in a safe place. They are good students, class leaders, athletes, etc. Yet there was an overwhelming feeling of anxiety that rested within them. Cody's suicide attempt gave them the freedom to have those discussions. It demanded it of them. As students came to drop letters

off to me it often turned into discussions. Some of these discussions ran long. On more than one occasion I had to ask a neighbor teacher to watch over my class so I could finish these discussions. I didn't want the kids to have to wait for anything when it came to this.

They were ready to talk and they needed someone to hear them. In some of these cases, I just happened to be the person they came to. Their stories were all unique. Other than the fear of having the discussion, there was no real common thread that ran through them. They came from both genders, all classes, students I knew well and others I didn't know as well. I spoke with athletes, speech and debate students, theater students, student leaders, you name the faction and I likely had a conversation with someone that identified with it.

He and other teachers were given a special opportunity to be part of a secret club, so to speak. One in which they were granted a glimpse into the students' world of emotional pain. Wade and the other teachers were given the privilege of their students' trust to hear their personal story and be part of the healing process. They were seeing the students' truth for the first time.

Those letters changed lives. People in our community started talking about depression, suicide and mental health. I could see crack after crack of light finding its way out of the darkness. Did I wish it wasn't our family that was the catalyst for this change? Yes, but not at the expense of what was happening all around us; I didn't want that to stop.

At the time, I had no clue this would bring Cody and our family into a world that desperately needed this story of hope. It was an overwhelming outpouring of love from our community. All from that dreaded letter that I didn't want to write or to be read, but knew it needed to be done. Healing was happening all around, and you couldn't ignore it.

12

THE AFTERSHOCKS

On the Sunday after the letter was read, close friends came over to check on us after we got back from our visit with Cody. My brother Gabe, Will and I were sitting on the back deck. I thanked them for all their support and help, and someone asked me, "How are you doing?" It was difficult for me to find a response, but what came to my mind was this, "I'm just so glad that Gabe is here to help plan Cody's future and not his funeral." And I remember Gabe looking at me and nodding his head in agreement. I held on to that as each day went on during this unmapped journey. I held on to that second chance.

I found that even though I was surrounded by loved ones, I felt alone in this pain. I don't think I could have escaped that, and I believe it was part of working through the crisis. I have heard people talk about how you can be in a room full of people and still feel alone when you are not around someone who has gone through what you have. I understood that now intimately; especially since no one really talks about suicide. This also meant Dana and Will had their own moments of loneliness and pain. Time felt like the enemy; I wanted the healing to move faster.

That night, Dana told us she wanted to go to school on Monday. She didn't have to, but needed to. Brave girl, and brave son – I was surrounded by bravery. Yet I wasn't brave enough to go to work and face people. We still didn't know the length of Cody's stay at the center and when he would be able to come home. There was still so much up in the air.

Dana got ready for school on Monday, and I kept asking her over and over if she was okay. I was stuck in the middle of not knowing what support she needed. Did she need me to tell her she didn't need to go, or did she need me to encourage her in the decision to go? I realized from watching her determined behavior when getting everything ready for school that she knew what she needed. I knew she was probably desperately seeking some normality in her routine. I followed her lead and gave her support and encouragement to make it through the school day.

We called Cody for our morning call and check-in, and told him we would visit after Dana got out of school. I called work to see how the upcoming race planning was going, and Media told me registrations were flying in. She said she thought we'd reach the goal of 500 this year. I was taken aback – that was great news. Wade called to set up a time to drop off a stack of letters for Cody. I used the rest of the day until Dana got home to catch up on house chores and bills. I wanted to stay busy so I didn't worry about Dana's first day back since the letter had been read.

When she got home, I tried to act calmly, asking her details about her day, but inside I was a mess of emotions. She said it was okay. She said everyone seemed nice, but she couldn't tell who knew or didn't know, so she just focused on school. I thought to myself, as she was talking, *I hope she's telling me the truth. I hope someone wasn't mean to her or teased her.* I was finding it difficult to trust what people were telling me. I worked at getting to her emotions and mental well-being by asking more specific questions to help her define what she was feeling. She just said it was a weird day, but it felt good to be there and she wanted to keep going. I let it be at that point. I knew counseling was in her future and I needed to tread gently with her. This was going to be a day-by-day feat. I wished and didn't wish I could read her mind.

We went to visit Cody first and then planned to eat dinner after. It was nice listening to Dana share her day with him; I think it was just what she needed. Cody shared his newest discovery: patients ordered their food from the hospital cafeteria each day, and he had discovered that when he put ketchup down for a condiment that they would only give him one packet. So he had quickly learned to order ketchup at each meal so he had extras for the meals he wanted it for. He would order ketchup with pancakes, with pasta, or even with a sandwich. We laughed at what the kitchen employee must have thought.

Cody shared more of what he was learning. He particularly enjoyed the group sharing sessions and getting to know the other patients. These continued to show him he wasn't alone, and it helped to hear their personal stories and share his.

I pulled out the letters that Wade had given me. He was always shocked by how many there were, but so excited to receive them. In the same moment, he would grab the stack of letters he had written in response to the letters he'd already received. We were acting as mail carriers, and I knew the words written in all these letters were part of everyone's healing process – it was something special.

While we were visiting, the nurse let us know that Cody's social worker would like a progress report meeting with all of us tomorrow. They planned it so we could go right into our mandatory parent meeting. Dana wouldn't be able to visit tomorrow, so we made sure this night's visit was as long as it could be.

Will, Dana and I said our goodnights, and headed to what had become our regular pizza place to eat at after visiting Cody. I hadn't had an actual appetite for a number of days, but I knew I needed to eat. For whatever reason, the only thing I wanted to eat was a slice of pizza and a Diet Coke. That may not sound strange, but it was for me; but even though my body was choosing those items to replenish itself was strange, I just went with it.

That night I was really missing Cody. Our dog would walk in and out of Cody's room and I could tell she knew something was amiss. Animals just know. I could hear Dana in the bathroom getting ready for bed. Usually the two of them would be joking and laughing. Those sounds were relaxing to me and helped me sleep, but for these last few nights, it had been Dana by herself, and I knew she must be missing her brother too. The house wasn't the same, our sounds were different – I wanted him home.

13

PUT ON A HAPPY FACE

Being a 4.0 student and a three-sport athlete with a
supportive family and good friends, I felt my external image
I put into the world did not match the reality of my health.
Cody Welty

Prior to our meeting with the social worker, we visited Cody. He showed us in more detail the surroundings of the center. This was a better tour than our first night, as we hadn't been in a good enough head space to absorb anything that night. He started the tour in the kitchen where he ate with other patients when he didn't eat in his room. It was a decent size room with a couple of big tables that could fit eight to ten people comfortably. Next, we walked into the open living room area where group therapy sessions were held; a couple of couches, overstuffed chairs and a coffee table were arranged throughout the open room. I could see a bookshelf that housed games, books, puzzles and magazines that the patients could use. As we walked around, Cody introduced us to staff and patients who crossed our path. It was nice to watch his interactions. He said his day consisted of group and individual therapy, education sessions, doctor visits, meal times and free time. He said he used his free time to write letters to people and the rest was spent doing treatment homework, journaling, shooting hoops or listening to music. His days were busy and productive.

The social worker was ready and waiting for us in the conference room. I had no idea what to expect. I was nervous. This wasn't your typical school conference where you get to hear about his progress in school and what a pleasure he is as a student. This meeting would be reviewing Cody's medical and emotional progress; this was much more serious. We said our pleasantries and he got started.

He conveyed that Cody was progressing and responding to treatment very well. He believed Cody would be ready to go home on Thursday or Friday of this week. I could see the excitement in Cody's eyes. The social worker continued with his assessment. Cody was working very hard on his personal and emotional growth and development. His treatment team was excited about his progress; they would let us know their final recommendation by Wednesday night. Many questions surfed through my head and I needed some clarification. I asked what our next steps were, as parents, and how we would help Cody transition from being an inpatient to being at home. He explained that if the recommendation was to release Cody, then he could do the rest of his recovery at home. We would have an additional in-depth meeting once that decision was final, which would cover next steps, house rules and getting Cody set up for counseling. We would also need to set him up with a medical doctor to monitor his medications and his progress. He added that the parent class we were attending would also answer many of the questions I was having. *I hope so, because I have no idea what I'm doing and how this works*, I thought to myself. I put on the best confident face I could at the moment.

I left that meeting relieved and apprehensive. I wanted Cody home, but I was fearful. Was he ready? Were we ready? I didn't feel like I had enough knowledge or tools. How would I ensure his safety? So many questions and no black-and-white answers. I didn't like this land of the unknown. I wanted to know where all the quicksand was, I didn't want to be surprised. Let's be real, life is never normal and life is an unknown at times, but at that moment I wanted to go buy a baby monitor to put in his room.

Our visits continued with Cody each day. I noticed my body and mind would become more anxious as we got closer to the treatment center because I never knew for sure what to expect. It became normal to not feel normal. I would wonder if Cody had a good day. Had there been a setback? Was he still going to get to come home? Would he have to move to an extended stay center? The future became a place I didn't visit often – it caused too much anxiety. I used to be that person who always liked to make plans, but now I found myself not doing it because I couldn't handle the thought process. I made the decision to try to only focus on the day in front of me and if that seemed overwhelming, I'd focus on the hour, and if that was a no go, then just on the moment. I believe that was the first coping skill I learned.

Today, Cody was having a good day. He shared in more details about his emotional "triggers", and how to cope when faced with them. He learned that an emotional trigger is a type of response to an event, a person or anything else that can provoke a strong emotional response. Sometimes we are not even aware of what causes it. Cody was learning coping techniques. For example, change the scenery, play music, take a shower, talk, journal and, most of all, realize it was normal to have them.

Cody felt validated after continuing to hear more personal stories during the group sessions. He felt good sharing his story, because he knew it was helping other patients not feel alone. During one of the group sessions, Cody shared how he felt like he was putting on a happy face every day when he woke up, and wasn't showing his true self. From that session, one of the patients, who was also an amazing artist, drew Cody a picture he shared with us. The picture depicted an advertisement showing how you could buy a happy face to wear to get through your day. Cody felt that drawing captured exactly what he was trying to convey. And, coincidentally, one of today's advertisements for antidepressant medication shows a woman carrying around a happy face mask that she can put on when she's around other people. Who would have known? It made me ache for him.

He had been living every day in our home feeling so alone, in pain, and I was clueless. How could I process this in my mind? I'm glad Cody shared all this information, and I wouldn't want it any other way, but I was struggling with how to process it. I felt I had failed him miserably as a parent. This wasn't about me having a pity party, I was trying to find a place for this overwhelming pain.

It was time for our class, so we said our goodbyes and went to a conference room on the hospital campus. The class started to fill up with what I assumed to be the parents and family of patients who were in treatment with Cody. I looked around the room and noticed that everyone was somber – no one was talking, and the majority of us had our heads down. We looked like a sports team who had just lost the biggest game of the year.

A woman with a hospital name tag walked through the door with a stack of packets in her arms. She introduced herself and handed out a packet to each of us. She first described why we were all there: it was a mandatory parent meeting for all families who had someone in treatment. The goal was to educate and prepare us for the next steps after treatment. It was going to be a night of overwhelming emotions and information. She educated the group on different types of mental health conditions, including suicide thoughts. I just kept talking to myself, saying, *How did I not know this? Why did I not know this? People need to know this.*

After her presentation, she asked each family to introduce ourselves and say why we were there. That was the first time Will and I told our story, and it was to a group of strangers – but tonight they were our people. There was no rush for time, there were no interruptions, everyone was glued to each other's personal story. A box of tissues got rotated around the table, and as the night progressed these people didn't feel like strangers anymore. These stories were brutal to hear, but necessary. The next to go was a woman professionally dressed and who looked like she had just come from work. She introduced herself as a single mom and her adult daughter sat next to her. She talked about her son, who was in treatment. When she said her son's name, I immediately knew who he was – the person who drew Cody that picture. My heart connected with her. Her story was compelling and I realized how alone she must feel as a single mom, and I realized how much I appreciated Will sitting next to me. Walking through this by myself would have added a whole additional layer of fear.

The class was informative, and by the end many of my earlier questions had been answered and I knew where to get more relevant information. I was climbing a Mount Everest of information, but I had excellent guides leading me down the correct path. My internet surfing days were over.

The next morning, both of my brothers headed back home because they knew they couldn't be here when Cody came home. Our friends and family kicked in with a food train once my brothers were gone. They organized it all and knew we didn't want to talk with anyone yet, I wasn't ready.

The show of support was coming from everywhere. Wade let us know that the baseball and softball teams put Cody's jersey number 13 on the inside of hats, and the baseball team hung his jersey in the dugout. One of the parents sent us a picture of that image just before we were heading in to a visit with Cody. I fell apart in the parking lot because I knew that picture could have also been a show of support for a different outcome. The softball teams wore yellow ribbons in their hair one night as a shout out to Cody and suicide awareness. I didn't even know that yellow ribbons had that meaning. We were surrounded by love.

It had been a rough season in baseball for Cody, especially since he loved the game. As I've replayed the last six months in my head, I can see now how he was withdrawing from baseball.

He didn't feel he was successful or valued; he felt he was striving for something that in reality was never going to be attainable in that program. All of those thoughts didn't come out in one conversation or as directly as I am writing them now.

Cody would collect baseballs from any city we visited, and family would give him baseballs from the places they visited. He not only enjoyed the physical part of the game but the mental element, which served him well as a catcher. He played other positions too, but the catcher position was the one that fit the best. He was considered a calm player, whether behind the plate or at the plate batting. Baseball can be stressful, and there is a ridiculous amount of politics between parents and coaches, especially since there are only nine spots on the field.

I had had a meeting prior to May 1st with the Athletic Director expressing Cody's frustration of being called out in practice, and that we felt there was inconsistency within the program. But being who Cody is he didn't want the AD to raise it with the coaching staff. I asked the AD that day to keep an eye on Cody. I have never had to go and talk to any teacher or coach about either one of my children, so the AD knew something was up when I requested a meeting.

The amount of regret I have for not taking further action is something I have carried, and I have had to walk through forgiving myself. I never thought what Cody was struggling with would have the outcome it did. As parents, we try to read every cue, from hormones to growing pains. Then you add the pressure of school, sports, and bring in relationships, and it can be difficult to decipher what may be happening. But I can tell you for certain that I never thought he could be depressed. *That* I wasn't thinking about. My phone rang and brought me back from my thoughts. It was the call I was waiting for: Cody was coming home tomorrow. I put my face in my hands and cried.

14

THE HOMECOMING

I didn't sleep much the night before Cody's return home as the same thoughts played in my head even though I did my best to silence them. I woke up with a mission. I wanted to clean Cody's room, give the dog a bath, and we desperately needed groceries. Dana decided to go to school to help her day go faster, plus she knew we had a meeting with the doctors and the social worker which she wasn't allowed to attend. She did, however, know that when she got home from school, Cody would be there.

I was relieved, excited and apprehensive. I knew Cody was ready to be home with his family, see our puppy, sleep in his own bed and have home cooking. I, however, lacked confidence and trust in my parenting ability. Having him home also had its fears.

The social worker was ready for us when we arrived. Will and I sat in his office for the first time. It was small, but cozy and comfortable. Many books were piled on his desk. He again conveyed the confidence that Cody's team felt he was ready to come home. He had responded to treatment well and felt he could continue his treatment plan at home. He discussed that we would need to develop house rules.

I jumped right in and said, "Like, I don't want his bedroom door closed at night."

He smiled at me and said, "Yes."

I jumped in again and said, "That he has to respond to all my calls and texts."

He just smiled again and nodded. I guess you could say I was nervous. He further explained that Cody needed to practice his coping skills to help improve his reactions to his triggers. This would require daily practice. He said we would get to go into more detail when we met with Cody prior to his discharge. He emphasized the need for all of us to be in counseling. I asked who was going to be Cody's counselor and he said that was up to us. Well, my heart skipped a beat. I made the assumption that he would have a counselor suggestion for Cody, but he didn't, that was left up to us. As he was talking I thought to myself, *Crap. I should have asked that earlier. Now I am behind. I didn't know I needed to find a counselor. I bet I also need to find a doctor to manage his depression medications*, which he confirmed in his next sentence. *Well, crap, now I'm really behind.* I was frustrated and a little panicked.

It was time for Cody to join our meeting; we gathered in the same conference room as when we arrived for his intake. The social worker updated Cody on everything we had already talked about, and then we started working on the house rules. This was a collaborative effort. We agreed that all they were for a point in time and could be reworked, added to or deleted. My top three were: keeping his bedroom door ajar when napping or at bedtime, checking his phone periodically and making sure Cody was never alone. I had already asked my neighbors, who are basically a second family to Cody, if, while I was at work, Cody could hang with Nicole, since she worked at home. Cody had no problem with that arrangement and understood my concerns. I had so many more rules I wanted, but I knew I was being over the top. Next, we talked about school. Cody didn't want to change schools and his goal was to get back before the end of the year. We would work with his doctor (the one we didn't have yet) to work toward that goal. The social worker then listed his required items for Cody. He needed to have a mentor who he would meet with once a week for an undetermined length of time. It should be someone outside the family. Cody wanted to ask Wade, and we all agreed with that choice. Wade had already offered to be of any assistance we needed with Cody so we were confident he would want to do this. Next were the proper steps to reintroduce Cody to family and friends. The guidance was to have one visit per day only with his closest family and friends; the visits shouldn't be longer than 20 minutes to start. I soon learned from Cody's body language during visits when he was getting tired and needed a break.

I had one last item to discuss – his car. I was honest and said I couldn't have it back. Cody felt the same way, and we agreed that our friend would sell it and the money would be used on a different vehicle. The social worker suggested we perform a family ritual when Cody got home, of burning a photo of the car as a way to say goodbye and move on. We took his advice on that.

It was now time to celebrate the exciting news of Cody coming home. We wrapped up the meeting by going over Cody's at-home plan, Cody shared with us his triggers and how he planned to cope, and we had a daily schedule of activities. There would be daily exercise, meditation, music, seeing a friend or family member once a day, and journaling his thoughts and feelings. Once I had got his counselor and medical doctor set up, his home treatment plan would be complete.

We went to his room and packed up everything. He left all the extra ketchup he got in the room for the next patient. He put his initials inside the closet, where other patients put theirs – he had shown us that earlier. He cheerfully said goodbye to the staff and other patients, and we walked out. I couldn't leave fast enough. It was a beautiful, sunny day with clear blue skies. I looked at Cody and noticed him looking all around with a big smile on his face.

I asked him what he was thinking and he said, "Everything is beautiful."

We got in the car and, like any teenage boy, Cody said, "I'm hungry." We all chuckled.

He decided on Wendy's, because it was close and a hamburger sounded good. During our drive he was looking around everywhere and kept commenting on how beautiful everything was. He was so grateful for treatment, but even more grateful that he was going home with so much more knowledge about his depression. He seemed free in his expressions and his ability to share what was on his mind came easier.

After lunch, as we took the 45-minute drive home, he shared what he was looking forward to. He wanted to see Dana and the puppy; he wanted to take a shower in his bathroom and sleep in his own bed. He was overflowing with gratitude. He talked about all the letters he got and how he was going to continue to write to everyone who wrote to him. That continued for a long time. Years later, I talked to one of his friends who received one of Cody's letters. She said to this day, she carries that letter in her wallet. I don't know what she wrote to Cody and I don't know what Cody wrote to her, all I know is that it must have been powerful.

I focused all my thoughts on good things, but knew I was vulnerable to fearful thoughts. *Could I do everything Cody and Dana needed to get well? Could I continue to work? Would we get him back to school? What if he wanted to go out with his friends or to a friend's house?* For today, hope pushed all that fear down.

Dana was still at school when we got home, but our cream-colored dog Cocoa, who is part cocker spaniel and Lhasa Apso, was home. She was lying on the carpet in the family room when she heard the door open. She immediately knew it was Cody. She could barely contain herself as her little legs scampered across the floor to him as he ran to her. He dropped to the floor and she just loved him. Then, when Cody just started walking around the house, Cocoa kept following him. Afterward, he walked back to me and gave me a huge hug. At that moment I started to see things I hadn't seen since elementary school. These were glimpses into his younger self before the world took hold, before depression took hold. Cody was still in there, he just needed the right help to set him free and we needed the right tools to help him. His laugh was back too, the kind of laugh that shows you don't care what people think. It was a powerful epiphany for me – a time of reflection, a learning moment. This was something tangible I could share with others someday; it was as if the day I almost lost my son was the beginning of his comeback.

Dana came through the door and Cody grabbed her and hugged her with both arms and hers around him. Her face laid on his chest as his chin rested on top of her head. Their smiles will forever be imprinted on my heart. I have no idea what they were both thinking, but the feeling of pure joy was all over their faces. It warmed my heart as an avalanche of emotions began to overtake me. I cherished the moment in front of me – my family was back together and I celebrated the homecoming.

15

THE COUNSELORS

The first night Cody was home was a night of tossing and turning in my bed. Although I was overjoyed that he was home and had thought I would sleep better, I realized my brain had a whole new set of worries. When he was in treatment, he was under constant watch, but at home that was impossible. My mind must have been trying to reconcile my fears in my sleep because I had two disturbing nightmares. After the first one, I woke up Will and asked him to check the whole house. After the second one, I didn't wake Will up – I lay in bed convincing myself it was a dream, but I couldn't let it go. I finally got up, angry that I couldn't get my fear under control. I went and stood outside Cody's bedroom door. His door was ajar like we agreed, but I was terrified to go in. I knew it was a dream, but my reality skills were not working properly, and I had never experienced fear that could stop me from moving before. I forced myself to gently open the door and walk a few steps into his room, from where I could see him lying on his back sound asleep; I could hear him breathing. I sighed and slowly tiptoed out. I went and checked on Dana, who was sound asleep. *It's okay Angie, it's going to take time*, I reassured myself as I sat at the top of the stairs outside Dana's room; I needed a minute to gather myself before heading back to bed.

That bedroom check became a private ritual I needed to do. Sometimes I would sit at the top of the stairs and pray.

Sometimes I fell asleep right there. I needed to be close to them. I did that off and on for months. Will kept my secret and never said a word to the kids, nor did he try to convince me to stop – it would have been impossible anyway, and he knew it helped me sleep better.

The next morning, Dana headed to school and Will went to work. I still had a few days before I had to be back at work, and I needed to focus on getting counseling and doctor appointments set up. Cody was still sleeping, so I took the opportunity to get started. The social worker had shared a psychology website that provided a list of counselors in our area. Our medical insurance provided counseling benefits, so between those two resources I felt confident that I would find the right counselor. Our insurance company gave me a list of providers within our plan, and also provided a name of a medical doctor close to us that specialized in mental health, who had great reviews. I called his office first and was grateful he was accepting new patients, it was just difficult to explain to the receptionist why I was calling. I wasn't used to fumbling over my words. They had an opening for next week and asked that his files from the treatment center be sent over.

Next, I had to find a counselor. Cody had said he would prefer a guy. I started with reading the bios of the psychologists from both lists and tried to highlight a few. It was difficult – I was looking at their pictures and trying to determine if they looked nice. I read and reread their experience, treatment style and hobbies to see if I felt it was a good match for Cody. Some were in private practice and some were attached to a counseling center. I decided to call the two from our insurance's counseling center who looked like a good fit. I explained my situation to the receptionist who proceeded to tell me that those two counselors were booked up for six to eight weeks and the majority of the others were also busy for the next four weeks. She said she could put me on a waiting list – that didn't go over well with me.

I said to her, "Maybe you don't understand the seriousness of our situation. We can't wait four to eight weeks for a counselor. Do you not have time set aside with these counselors for emergency situations?"

She replied with a flat, "No."

She didn't even say, "No, I'm so sorry." Her demeanor was cold, as though she gets calls like this every day. My response was one of frustration that no counselor was available but more so for her lack of compassion. My voice was cracking and tears were flowing. She could hear in my voice that she had struck a nerve and tried to rally by providing me the telephone number to a county mental health office where I may be able to find some help. I hung up and threw our cordless phone onto the couch. My emotions were raw. I gathered myself and called the number she gave me. They specifically dealt with immediate crisis situations and would be more than willing to talk with Cody if he was really struggling, but they didn't have counselors on site for continued counseling services. She was nice, empathetic and tried her best to help. She provided an emergency number in case Cody did reach a crisis point. I hung up the phone defeated. I closed my eyes and prayed; I wasn't coping well.

I decided to go back to my original list of private counselors: some were within our insurance and some were not. At this point, I didn't care. Three made my list. Two were older and had years of experience, but their pictures didn't speak to me. The second was in private practice and didn't take insurance, but his face spoke to me. He was younger and I thought Cody might relate to him better. I was torn. Do I go with more experience or with a youthful connection? I asked Cody and he said he would be fine with anyone I thought looked good. Ugh, I didn't want to mess this up.

I chose experience, and guess what? Those two were fully booked and not accepting patients. What was going on? I felt so helpless and anxious that I couldn't find anyone. I didn't think it would be this hard. I made a call to the counselor whose face had spoken to me. I was pacing outside on my deck when I made the call. It must have been his private cellphone number because it went straight to his personal voicemail – no one was screening his calls. I left a detailed jumbled message. I wished I could have redone that message – my explanation of our situation was all over the place. I finally stopped pacing and sat down on our deck steps. I told myself to let it go. Now, I waited.

Once Cody was awake, I let him know about the doctor's appointment and the struggle in finding a counselor. I was completely honest about the experience and how I misunderstood the social worker, so I felt behind in getting his treatment set up. He reassured me he was doing okay.

I looked at him and said, "Cody, I know you tell me that but I don't know if that is the truth."

He understood, and we both agreed this was going to take time to rebuild trust. It felt good to speak so honestly with each other. The phone rang as we were wrapping up our conversation. I could tell by the number that it was the counselor returning my call. I walked back outside and answered the call.

"This is Angie," I said, trying to sound calm.

He introduced himself and said he had listened to my message and wanted to hear more about Cody's situation. His voice was pleasant and sounded sincerely interested in helping Cody. *Was I hearing this right? My voice message made sense to him and he was interested in helping Cody?* I hesitantly asked if he had an opening for next week and he said yes. I audibly sighed with relief and immediately relaxed. He asked me for some more detail regarding Cody's inpatient experience along with the recovery goals. I didn't get far into the details when I started to choke up. The emotional pressure of finding a counselor was releasing, and I couldn't get it under control. I paused and asked for a minute to regain my composure. He understood. I started again and he calmly, without ever interrupting me, listened to my mess of a description of Cody's story. He expressed his sincere desire to work with Cody, and then shared some history about himself and how he felt he could help Cody. The more he talked, the more I connected with him. I believed his background would speak to Cody. He explained he wasn't in a place to take insurance yet, but adjusted his rates to account for that. I didn't care that we didn't have insurance coverage, I believed that would work itself out; I couldn't schedule the appointment fast enough. I hung up the phone and immediately came in to tell Cody. He seemed excited too. Cody's team was complete, now I needed Dana's.

Getting Dana a counselor proved much easier as there were so many more female psychologists available. I knew Dana had lost trust in this world, and her once carefree soul had started to carry a burden of exactly what, I didn't know. I wanted her to believe in the good and begin to trust again, but I knew painfully well that I couldn't stop this process for her, no matter how much I wanted to. I couldn't protect her from the pain. I couldn't protect her from the looks of teachers or students or family or friends. What I could do was find a counselor who could help her learn the tools to cope and be her advocate. Her person, who she could rely on and trust. I narrowed down a list for Dana, and then she looked at the pictures and bios. We decided on two who looked good. I was able to get our first choice and booked an appointment for two weeks' time.

Will and I scheduled our appointment for three weeks' time with our previous marriage counselor. We had had success with him and he knew our family and fit us into his schedule quickly. I tried to space all the first appointments out to allow me to give my full attention to each session. It was going to be busy, but I was glad – progress was happening.

Now Cody and I focused on his daily at-home treatment schedule, along with setting up his first family and friend visits. Everyone was anxious to see him, but we were committed to moving slowly.

16

RINSE AND REPEAT

If you have seen or heard of the movie *Groundhog Day* you know it is about a guy who gets trapped in a time loop and relives the same day every day – that was how Cody and I spent our days together in the beginning.

His daily at-home treatment plan started with exercise. Being a personal trainer and group exercise instructor for many years paid off as we did all sorts of bootcamp-style workouts. My boss from the gym let me borrow a weight bag and gloves so Cody could mix up the workouts with boxing and sparring drills. We incorporated yoga and Pilates, and finished his workouts with meditation. The rest of his day would be spent on private journaling, writing letters to students and family, and one family or friend visit a day. Once counseling and doctors' appointments started, they too became part of our weekly schedule.

Cody's first visit happened to be with one of the families that Cody had grown up with since birth. Cody and I developed a list of topics that he would be willing to talk about and ones that he wasn't. He didn't mind repeating stories, or being asked the same questions. He was more afraid of trying to carry the conversation. Before each visit, I prepped the family or friends on the topics they could bring up and what to stay away from. They also knew I was sticking to a strict 20-minute visit rule. The question they all asked was if it would be okay to hug him; the answer was yes. Cody needed that hug too, and he understood why they did.

Cody was nervous for his first visit, but knew it was part of his recovery process, and he was excited to begin to see his friends and family.

Once the family had arrived and lots of hugs had been exchanged, we sat in the family room. My job was to help direct conversation as needed and look for any signs that Cody wasn't doing well. I didn't know what those were yet, and knew this would be trial and error. Cody was doing as well as I could tell, but one of his knees was bouncing up and down quickly. He was anxious – so was I. If you could have seen my heart, it was probably beating just as fast as his knee. We both knew this was going to be tough, but I had to let the visit play out; we had to start somewhere. The family did a wonderful job of keeping the conversation light and flowing. Just before the 20 minutes was up, I spoke up and said it was time to say goodbye as we didn't want to push these visits too long for Cody. They understood with no hesitation. Cody felt relieved after that first visit, and so did I. He was glad to see people, and was focused on doing what was necessary to get well.

The visits continued for weeks and, each time, the anxiety reduced. Seeing our close family was very emotional. It was hard for everyone not to be overly emotional, so we just let the emotions happen and didn't try to squash them. Cody was able to hug whoever was struggling. With each visit I learned something new about Cody's time in treatment or his recovery thoughts, whether it be a new funny story or a more detailed discussion about his triggers. One visit was particularly difficult for me.

Wade had come for his weekly mentor meeting and Cody started to share how baseball had become a trigger. He had reached a point where he didn't want to play and dreaded practice. As he was describing his feelings, his hand started to shake like it did in the ER and when we made the long walk to the treatment center. I looked at him and he saw the concern in my eyes. He told me it was okay; he wanted to have a team visit, and to be able to do that he needed to work through his emotions. Wade was clear back to him: his teammates wanted to see him.

He continued talking and shared how he was bullied during football. Wade and I both began to tear up. Rage began to build inside of me and I was desperately trying to control my facial expression. My pulse was racing and I felt the need to scream at these people. I didn't know these stories he was telling.

Cody must have read my face because he said, "Mom, I'm sorry I didn't tell you. I was trying to take care of it myself."

"I'm so sorry Cody this happened to you. I'm so grateful we're talking about it now," I replied.

But inside, I was screaming at myself and my guilt was growing. Playing any future sports was a question mark. My only focus was getting him well and, if possible, back to school before the end of the year.

As the visits continued over the weeks, Cody didn't need me to start conversations or to sit in on every one, especially those with his friends. He wanted more privacy with them, and I understood. They would go to the game room. Some of my most precious moments were when his friends came over to see him, because they always made sure to give me the biggest hug and tell me how much they loved our family. I needed those hugs. I was exhausted and living with so much guilt that their hugs and words fueled my tank. I began to notice Cody's passion for educating everyone on depression and mental illness. He would explain what had happened to him, what he had learned. Everyone listened intently – not out of respect for Cody, but because they were learning something they didn't know much or anything about. Without Cody even knowing, he was becoming an advocate for mental health awareness and education right there in our living room.

17

A NOT-SO-NORMAL WEEK
IN THE NEIGHBORHOOD

My first official day back at work coincided with Cody's first counseling session. I had worked out a schedule where I worked half days as this allowed flexibility with the counseling and doctor appointments. As I was going to be at work, we had to put into action the new house rule that, for a while, Cody would hang out with Nicole, our friend. We had a few laughs about this to bring some lightheartedness to the situation. It obviously wasn't typical to send your 17-year-old son to the neighbor's house to be watched while Mom went to work, but it gave me peace.

While at work, I tried to focus on the final preparations for my upcoming race, but my head kept floating back to home and worrying about my family. And while I was at home, I would worry about work. It was a constant battle to stay put in one place in my mind. Media and staff had everything covered regarding the race, but as the director there are always last-minute decisions to make. Registrations were flooding in and I had an overabundance of people from the community wanting to know if they could be volunteers for the race. It was an outpouring of love and I didn't know how to handle it. I was given a tremendous amount of support at work – they shielded me from club members when necessary and allowed me the privacy to cry in the office upstairs. I cried at work more times than I did at home; I didn't want the kids to see all my emotions. These managers knew me and my family closely – that gym was my kids' second home. They understood that I could be fine one minute and crumbling the next. I realized how jealous I was of Will during this time. He could go to work where no one knew what had happened and could get a mental and emotional break.

While at work, Nicole would send me text messages on how Cody was doing. She knew I needed an update every now and then. I tried not to text Cody all the time, so her check-ins helped. I think at times we had an ESP connection – just when I would be wondering about him, I'd get a text or picture from her. Before I even decided to go back to work, Nicole and I had talked and made this arrangement for Cody. I realized I was asking a lot of my friend, and I didn't want to put her in an uncomfortable situation. We were both concerned about Cody's safety, and we wanted to believe him when he said he wasn't having thoughts of suicide. All we could do was hope we were seeing the true Cody who was being honest with us. I will forever be grateful to Nicole and Scott for all they did for our family.

After I got home from work, Cody and I sat down and got ready for his counseling appointment. We were both anxious for different reasons. I was concerned Cody would not like him, and was apprehensive about his experience and level of expertise regarding suicide. Cody had an overall nervous feeling and couldn't pinpoint exactly why. It only took us 15 minutes to get to his office. The counselor had let me know his building was originally a house, which he had converted into an office. I was told to enter via the side door and take a seat in the waiting room; he would get us at the time of our appointment. We found the building no problem, and it was exactly as he had described. We parked and walked in via the side door. You entered into a foyer with a bathroom on the left and a small hall that led directly to the waiting room, which looked like it must have been a living room before. It was simply decorated with a nice picture window that faced a busy street where you could hear traffic going by. Artwork hung on the walls, a number of wooden chairs were available to sit in, and magazines were lined up on a table. A little table housed a place to get bottled water, coffee and tea. We sat down next to each other and began to whisper simple conversation back and forth. The counselor had given us some paperwork to complete prior to the session, so I pulled that out and had Cody review it one more time.

Within about ten minutes, his counselor walked into the room. He had the most pleasant and easy-going personality. I could tell an instant connection between him and Cody had occurred. We were both invited into his office. Cody and I sat spaced on a comfortable couch that was placed against the wall opposite the counselor's wingback chair. There was another overstuffed chair in the room, which was next to a window with sheer curtains that let in the light but kept the room private. The lighting was soft, and there was a nice smell in the office, but I couldn't tell you the scent. His diplomas hung on the wall behind him and a clock was placed where we could both see the time.

After further introductions, we reviewed the paperwork and counseling protocols. The counselor felt it was important for me to be there during the first few visits because family would be an important part of Cody's recovery. After that, I would be pulled in as necessary. I knew Cody needed privacy to speak freely. We all knew it had to be the right balance. The counselor then asked Cody and me to tell him our story. It was the first time I heard Cody tell it in his own words, and it was the first time he heard me talk about it. The appointment lasted an hour and a half and flew by. We both were exhausted by the end.

Counseling would be twice a week and Cody was given an assignment before we left; the counselor wanted to know what some of Cody's goals were. For example, Cody wanted to get back to school before the end of the year and he wanted to see his baseball team.

On the drive home, I waited patiently for Cody to tell me what he thought. We didn't even reach the end of the street when he said he really liked him. I noticed that the 50lb invisible weight I felt on my shoulders lifted, along with the tiger-like grip I had on the steering wheel. I was so relieved. For the rest of the drive home we listened to music – we both needed to decompress and that worked for us because we both love music. There is nothing like jamming to music with your kid in the car, and that became our post-counseling ritual.

That same week, Cody had his first appointment with the medical doctor who would be monitoring his antidepressants, his depression levels and any other mental health concerns.

We learned so much on this visit and both liked the doctor. Cody had to complete a mental health questionnaire which set his baseline on a point scale. We were told that at each visit he would complete the same questionnaire in order to monitor his progress. After introductions and the telling of Cody's story, we went over his inpatient treatment file and medication list. Next, he asked us to watch a video that explained how depression affects the brain and how his current medication Celexa works to help his brain heal. That video answered so many of my questions regarding depression and the brain, and how medication works. Cody and I were both glued to the video. It made me want to get home and learn about the science of depression and treatment. It helped me understand how medication assists in the treatment of not only depression but other mental health conditions. That was a crucial moment for me; medication treatment had always scared me. Growing up with an alcoholic father made me wary of taking anything that may be addictive, but now I could see the important relationship between medication and therapy in a recovery process. There is no one road to recovery. There are hits and misses along the way, but at least we were trying to swing. It is the same with a counselor and medication. If one counselor doesn't work for you, try another. If a medication doesn't work, maybe your body needs a different combination. For Cody, medication was necessary, but so was counseling. Cody had monthly appointments with his doctor to monitor his overall progress and any side effects of the antidepressants. Of course, we could call at any time if we felt Cody wasn't doing well. Cody finally talked about his struggle with getting to sleep, and he was prescribed a very light, non-habit-forming medication to try to help get his sleeping pattern established. Once established, he could continue on the melatonin that he used while in treatment, and only return to the other medication if he hit a rough patch with sleep. We left there feeling a greater understanding of mental illness and medication, but most of all we had even more hope for recovery.

18

MOTHER'S DAY

Mother's Day felt different this year; my mind would jump from being incredibly grateful to imagining the worst-case scenario. I continued to force myself to believe what I saw within Cody to be true, but I didn't want to ever fall as hard as I had and I didn't ever want to be fooled again.

I wanted a low-key, stay-at-home barbecue dinner with my family. We hadn't been going out in public much and this was definitely not a day on which I wanted to run into people. Nevertheless, this ended up being a Mother's Day to remember.

It started when I walked out of our doorway and down a few steps into the garage – there was a beautiful hanging pink petunia basket with a card gently laid on top. I looked outside our open garage doors but couldn't see any cars around. I leaned over, grabbed the card and sat down on the steps. It was a Mother's Day card from one of Cody's best girlfriends and her family. The words written inside made me cry – a sweet and thoughtful expression of love. I took the basket and card inside to share with everyone. Will immediately found a hook outside to hang the basket from and I enjoyed looking at it while I finished my coffee.

A few hours later, while eating lunch, the doorbell rang. Will immediately said he would get it, knowing the rest of us weren't up to visitors. He opened the door and then asked me to come to the front door. I was apprehensive because I didn't want to try and make conversation with anyone. As I walked toward the door, I saw Will pointing down at the doormat. Sitting there was a beautiful bouquet of bright-colored flowers in a dark rose-colored vase; a card was tipped up against it. Will hustled down our walkway to see who had delivered it, as I sat down on the front porch step and opened the card. Will walked back and said he caught a glimpse of Carson's car driving away. Carson was one of Cody's childhood friends who he played baseball with. It was another Mother's Day card and the words written within about a mother's love spoke directly to my soul. He had signed it, "The Baseball Team and Carson." It was so unexpected. Neither one of these friends realized how much their acts of kindness meant to me and my pained heart. I was severely struggling with feelings of letting my children down. The tears started coming and I knew I wasn't going to be able to stop them. I quickly took the flowers, placed them on our kitchen island, and shared the cards with the kids before heading out to our back deck. As I fell into our rattan chair, I let my confused emotions come to the surface and started sobbing uncontrollably. At some point, Will had quietly come and sat next to me. He just let me cry; he didn't know what to do to comfort me.

I was feeling strong emotions of joy and hope, more than I realized possible. I don't believe I experienced the true power and depth of each of those emotions until everything happened with Cody.

On the flip side, the power and ugliness of fear was looming around me. It was as if it was waiting for the right time to engulf me during my most vulnerable state. I used to believe I could handle or face almost anything. I realize that sounds ridiculous, but it was what I had told myself to get through my childhood trauma, and it worked. It wasn't working now though. This fear was different, it was merciless, it was kicking my butt. I wasn't doing well, even though I had joy and hope in my corner. I couldn't put my finger on the exact issue, it was hidden in the mayhem of my competing emotions. The tears that were now flowing were necessary. I needed to get at the root cause – but it wouldn't happen today.

I was in a fully fledged hysterical crying fit when Cody opened the slider to the deck and said with an awkward expression on his face, "Mom and Dad. The Deputy Sheriff who was with me on May 1st knocked on the door and is here to check on us. He's making his way to you on the deck."

Cody had answered the front door when he heard the knock, because he knew his dad and I were on the back deck and that I wasn't doing very well.

In complete shock, I replied, "What? Oh geez Cody, I'm so sorry. That had to have been scary opening the door and seeing him." I barely had enough time to get the statement out before the Deputy was at our back deck.

If you only could have seen me, I was a blubbering mess. My contacts were blurry and I could barely see because of all the crying. My head was pounding, and I desperately needed a tissue. I must have been quite the sight for the Deputy, let alone the young ride-along he had with him.

The Deputy looked at us with a questioning expression, and gently asked how we were all doing. There was no question how physically bad I looked at that point, but I didn't care. I stood up and hugged him anyway. I explained what had just happened and why I looked the way I did. We all chuckled at the timing of his visit. We spent the next 10 to 15 minutes having a nice visit and updating him on Cody. He was happy to see him doing better.

We walked the Deputy to his patrol car and, as he drove off, Cody put his arm round me and asked if we could be done with the day. I nodded in total agreement. It was a Mother's Day I will always remember.

19

COUNSELING AND MORE COUNSELING

My Run Girlfriend Run race day arrived and Cody knew, emotionally, he couldn't be there. There would be too many people, too many looks, and he wasn't ready. I agreed, but I was going to miss him. The day was a success, with 444 runners, my biggest event yet. I was exhausted and relieved it was over. The younger daughter of a friend of mine asked her mom if something was wrong with me, she said I didn't look right. Her daughter didn't know what had been happening with my family, yet she could see something was off. She was right – I was on autopilot and not emotionally present. I started that fundraising race years ago for my daughter; I had wanted to show her how strong women are, share my love of running and teach her how important it is to give back.

This Run Girlfriend Run scholarship fund was my passion, and I wanted to share it, but right now my passion bank was empty and I was fighting to be in the moment. I was keenly aware of how many times I searched for Dana among the crowd; I needed to see how she was doing. This would be the first time since May 1st that she would be seeing a number of her friends, and their families too. I was concerned she would get stuck in a conversation she didn't want to have. I had asked my sister to help me keep an eye on her, since I was going to be pulled in many directions at the event. Dana was my main motivation for getting through the day, and I wanted it to be good for her.

Next week was the start of her counseling sessions and I knew she was apprehensive, so I wanted the race to be the start of a good week for her.

The race was a success, with no hiccups. It was a great example of teamwork and having wonderful volunteers and sponsors. I know they were not all there for the race, but to help me and my family. I was grateful and felt I could rest now, at least for a day before Dana's appointment.

Prior to Dana's appointment we talked about what to expect during her first visit. I shared how the counselor would probably ask questions to help her start. I told her it was okay to share anything she wanted, including if she was angry, disappointed or upset with me, Dad or Cody. It was her safe place to begin her healing journey. I did let her know that I would most likely sit in for part of the first visit to help communicate details regarding Cody and to understand the counselor's treatment plans and learn how she would like us to support Dana. I second-guessed every conversation I was having with Dana, hoping I was covering everything. At times, I was over-communicating information, but I was afraid if I didn't tell her something, it may cause her more trauma. I had no idea what the right balance was. I was feeling my way through an unmarked jungle without a guide and without the right tools, while trying to protect her. It was terrifying.

Counseling day came, and Dana and I headed out for the 20-minute drive into town, keeping conversation light. Dana's counselor was part of a team of counselors with a larger service provider. Her office was located on an upper floor of a professional, brick office building. In the waiting room there were clients sitting in the chairs that lined three walls; the decor was warm, with typical pictures of scenery on the walls. There must be science behind which pictures of nature make you feel more comfortable.

The reception desk was to the right; we headed over to check Dana in. As per their instructions, we had arrived 20 minutes early to complete the required paperwork. Dana and

I found some seats and quietly started filling out the paperwork together. They also had a mental health check form for her to complete regarding how she was doing mentally. Every time I had to write the reason for the visit, "brother attempted suicide," and that made it more real because I could see those words in my own handwriting. Once we had finished, we turned in the paperwork and waited.

Trying to make conversation while waiting is awkward, but Dana and I did our best. It wasn't long before her counselor opened a door and called her name. I knew it was her because I had seen her picture on the website. We introduced ourselves, and she asked us to follow her down a hallway that had doors on each side. The doors had nameplates and some had small machines that were making white noise outside the door. *That must help with keeping conversations from being overheard*, I thought.

We arrived at her door and walked into a nicely decorated office with books throughout and a small couch and soft lighting. Dana and I sat down on the couch and her counselor sat in the chair across from us. The counselor got started by reviewing the paperwork we had completed and by asking us to describe why we were there. Even though that question is necessary, it's also strange because you never quite know where to start. It isn't like going to the doctor knowing you have a problem with your leg and having them take an x-ray to find out the problem. When the x-ray comes back, they can clearly see you have a broken leg and they know how to treat it – maybe with a cast, some crutches or physical therapy; there is a plan. With mental health it isn't always that clear. There is no way to x-ray the heart and soul of a person, see the specific problem, then cast it and wait for it to heal. I answered her question the best I could, then Dana spoke a little. I sat in for about 20 minutes before the counselor asked for time alone with Dana.

It was the same scenario as with Cody – I may or may not be needed during future appointments. I had noticed in those first

20 minutes that Dana seemed comfortable, but I would wait until I heard from Dana. I had no problem with trying to find a different counselor if needed.

I walked back into the waiting room and used the time to reflect. I had already noticed how quiet Dana was getting and it made me nervous. How could I blame her, she was looking at life through a new lens and it was foggy. This wasn't something I had prepared her for. Typically, Dana will sit back and evaluate any new situation before she engages, but this was a different type of quiet. She needed a place to download, she needed her own individual support, she needed to know that her family was going to be okay. However, I knew I couldn't guarantee that last statement.

I wanted to show Cody and Dana that nothing could break this family and we were all going to be okay, but I couldn't. That only works in the movies when you get to write your own script. When it comes to real life, all sorts of scenarios come into play and you start to question whether you can weather the storm together. It's important for me to be real here. I had no idea what our future held. I had had plans for our family prior to May 1st, but those plans were now on hold, maybe indefinitely, I didn't know. I hated not knowing. I hated not knowing if Dana was really okay, if Cody was really okay. I don't like the word hate, but I hated what was happening to them, and I hated depression, and I hated that I didn't know enough about mental illness.

My thoughts immediately stopped once I saw Dana walk back through the door. Her sweet face had a timid smile. I asked her how it went and if she liked the counselor. She said yes. A loud applause echoed through my head. Again, I was grateful. Dana had her person in place. We talked briefly about the appointment and then enjoyed our drive home. I didn't want Dana to feel pressured to tell me something she didn't want to or was not ready to tell me. We were both just feeling our way.

The next week Will and I had our first counseling appointment. It was strange to be there together not focusing specifically on our marriage, but more on getting the necessary tools to help our family. Our counselor was clear with us that many marriages have difficulty surviving crises of this nature, especially with the unknown of Cody's healing process. He said it takes a toll on a marriage and it's not unusual for one partner to move through the healing process quicker. I was pretty adamant with Will that we needed to get our crap together, because there was no way our children were going through any more than they had already. I almost felt panicked, and an overwhelming desire to control this outcome emerged.

What I discovered during this appointment was that the issues of my past counseling were rising to the surface with three times the power. My insecurities, fears, negative thoughts and past failures were ripping the layers of healed skin off of me. I kept saying I was handling everything, but my soul was telling me something different. I feared I was not strong enough to battle the waves of pain that wanted to overtake me. When I left counseling that day I told myself, *You must hold onto the lifebuoy of hope.*

20

THE OUTING OLYMPICS

Cody was ready to see his baseball team after working with his counselor for a few sessions. It was decided that only players, Will, myself and Wade would be at the meeting. The location would be at the home baseball field. Wade would manage the visit and keep the time short. This would be the first time the team had seen Cody since May 1st. It's a quick ten-minute drive to the field and my stomach was doing flips the entire way. Cody described it as a necessary part of his healing process. I called it a complete out-of-body experience; I could feel a tingling sensation in my body as I saw the team on the field and Wade waiting for us in the parking lot. Will parked, and we all got out of the car. There was a quick hello, a review of the process and then, just as quickly, Cody and Wade headed to see the team. The guys were so glad to see him, you could see it on each of their faces, just authentic emotions of joy. Hugging, laughing and normal teenage boy behavior. It was a sight. I tried to focus on Cody's face to read his behavior and comfort level. He seemed good.

Will and I waited next to the visitors' dugout – we wanted to give them space. The team had signed a baseball to give to Cody. Then they started doing some baseball fun drills; this was great because it didn't require Cody or his teammates to carry conversation – it was the perfect set-up. We wrapped up the visit and I could tell Cody was tired. As the boys and Cody were coming off the field, each player made it a point to hug Will and me. It was authentic and overwhelming. The visit was a success.

That week also included Dana's track meet. When I came to watch, I stayed close to Nicole. Her daughter was on track too. It was hard walking through the crowds because I felt like people were staring and talking about my family. You may say to yourself, *Don't let it get to you*, but in reality it does. You believe things are being said about you even though they might not be. The mind can be your friend and foe, and I was constantly having to work on shutting up that negative side of my head.

Since meeting with the team, Cody was working on his next goal of getting back to school. During Cody's counseling that week, they asked me to come in to discuss that possibility and what it looked like. We needed a plan we all felt comfortable with. We all agreed that getting a week or so of school in before the end of the year would be good. It would break the ice and help with the anxiety of seeing friends over the summer. Also, it would help with summer football if Cody did decide to participate and would put closure on this year of school. Cody expressed how he wanted to meet with his teachers first and explain what would be helpful for his transition back. His counselor felt it was important for the teachers to see Cody and for them to be able to ask questions directly prior to his return. I would join Cody during that meeting, so we all heard the same information and his teachers would be aware of the support Cody had at home.

Cody and I worked with Wade and Cody's school counselor, Seth, to get everything set up. A meeting was set for Friday May 30th, after school was out and most students were gone. Emails were sent to teachers, and the feedback was extremely positive. All Cody's teachers would be there, and they expressed in their emails their excitement to see Cody. Wade instructed us to enter through a back entrance by the library; this would limit the chances of Cody running into someone he wasn't ready to see.

I appreciated that sentiment because, a week earlier, when I had to have a meeting about Cody at the school, I wasn't prepared for the exposure. I had Wade there to greet me and walk with me to the meeting, but on my way out, I was solo. I ended up seeing a student in the hallway who knew me. Once she saw me she started crying. All I could do was give her a hug and try to get the hell out of there as fast as I could. I didn't want that to happen to Cody.

After that interaction, I tried to quickly check-out on the log book at the school front office when something caught my eye. It was the nameplate of the attendance secretary, who was sitting to the right of me behind her desk. She was the woman who called 911 for the cyclist who saved Cody – the one who told the sheriff that Cody was a good boy. I had never met her, and she had never met me. I couldn't help it, I walked over to her desk. Her head was down, she was wearing something floral and had short brown hair. She was close to my age.

"Excuse me," I said quietly.

The woman with the sweetest face and smile looked up to me from her computer and said, "Can I help you?"

I also noticed a woman out of the corner of my eye who was sitting at a workstation close to her, and who was now staring at me. *She must know who I am*, I thought.

I introduced myself to the attendance secretary, "My name is Angie Welty, and my son is Cody." Before I could say another word, the woman jumped from her seat and ran round her desk to hug me. I hugged her back and whispered, "Thank you so much." She started to cry and whispered back to me, "You are a good mother." I closed my eyes and took in her words. I had just received another piece of my puzzle – I now knew who she was.

We released our embrace. As I was saying goodbye and turned to leave, I was again unprepared for one of Cody's teachers to come straight up to me and hug me from out of nowhere. He whispered how sorry he was and nothing more. I thanked him, but could feel the walls starting to collapse around me – I just needed out. I proceeded to walk out of that school, holding my breath to stop me from sobbing. I was internally shoving the pain down with all my strength. The pain wanted out, but I had to make it to the car. I walked as fast as I could. *Why did I park so far away?*, I thought as I walked as fast as my short legs could take me. I slammed the car door shut and started pounding on my steering wheel sobbing. I didn't care if anyone saw me. *Start the car Angie, just start the car!* I took the longest way home possible. I needed time to calm down.

As I reflected back on that experience, I knew it was not something I wanted Cody to go through. I was all on board with giving Cody protection for this upcoming meeting.

Meeting day arrived and Cody was very well aware that it was going to be awkward. We arrived and met Wade at the side entrance. He walked us down a hallway into a conference room where his teachers and counselor were waiting. They got up and greeted us with hugs, smiles and tears. Cody and I took a seat next to each other and made light conversation as we waited for a couple of other teachers to arrive. Once everyone was there, Wade started the meeting.

The goal was to help Cody and his teachers with his transition back to school. The teachers knew that it wasn't about making up schoolwork, it was about helping him walk through the school doors and seeing and being with his peers. Wade then turned it over to Cody for him to explain what he was going through and what he needed going forward. Cody explained what he had learned in treatment about his triggers and the high level of expectations he felt, even though he wasn't sure, and didn't ask, what someone was really expecting of him. He explained that he was learning to ask those questions now, and hoped for open conversations with each of them.

He was brave to sit there with all these adults looking at him for answers. They were all committed to helping Cody succeed. They had a number of questions, specifically related to what to do if they felt concerned about him and his safety. Cody responded by saying to them to ask him directly. I chimed in and added that they were encouraged to let Wade or his counselor know if Cody seemed off, or even if they were just concerned. Cody understood everyone was on high alert.

The second question was about expectations. Cody encouraged them to be clear with him about their expectations and he agreed to ask clarifying questions. It wasn't about the difficulty of the assignment; it was more about the expectation. Cody let them know that he was planning to be at school the following Wednesday. This allowed a few days to soak in the information from today and see if they had any other questions or concerns before he arrived. Everyone felt good about the plan. Cody shared that he was planning to go to the girls Softball Championship Game on Saturday. He hoped it'd make coming back to school a little easier. This way he would see some students he hadn't seen during his home or baseball visits, and maybe prevent his first day back being such an event.

That Saturday, Cody, Will and I loaded into the car to head to Oregon State University for the Girls Softball 5A State Championship Game. The agreement was that if at any time Cody needed to leave, we would. We would also try to sit away from everyone. There were going to be a lot of teachers and students who Cody hadn't seen yet at this game.

We pulled into the gravel parking lot and immediately saw Bryce, a teammate from the baseball team. Bryce yelled hello and waved at Cody, obviously excited to see him. Cody waved back and smiled. My stomach started to hurt at this point – this was my first true outing, and I was nervous – I dug in my purse and found the Tums that I now kept on hand. We had no idea how Cody was going to do, but we had to face these unknowns to heal. I had always taken for granted the ins and outs of normal life and how you operate without worry.

We started walking to the stadium. I was so glad I had my sunglasses on. This way no one could make eye contact with me. If someone waved I waved back, but otherwise, I went stealth. We walked up a staircase to enter the stadium at the top. The bleachers were below. I started to scan the bleachers for a place to sit out of the way. At that moment, Cody caught sight of Bryce standing up and waving to him to come sit with him. Bryce was sitting with all the players from Cody's baseball team at the bottom rows close to the first base line. Cody looked at us, smiled and headed down to the team. Will and I, however, looked at each other and realized, *Oh crap! So much for the plan*, even though Cody's choice to be with his friends was a thousand times better than the plan.

In all the commotion, we noticed people staring at us, and I froze. Thank God, at the same nanosecond that I was frozen, a baseball parent couple stood up and waved us over to sit by them. I was being rescued and couldn't have been more grateful, but I was still frozen. Will had to physically grab my hand to get me to move. We walked down and they reached out and hugged us quickly and sat down. They must have sensed my fear because they quickly started to make normal conversation with us. They shared how good it was to see us. Then, we just sat and enjoyed the game like any other normal day. From where I sat, I could see Cody clearly and was prepared for the possibility that at any instant he would either come over or send me a text to say he was ready to go. However, that never happened. He was smiling and cheering, and my heart and soul, for those two and half hours, were at peace. Those boys cared for him and he cared for them. It was his baseball family, and ours too.

The softball team won that day, and so did all of us. The rest of the boys went down on the field to congratulate the girls, but at this point, Cody was ready to go. This actually provided a nice way for to exit quietly as the celebration was going on. We got into the car and celebrated all the wins that happened that day on our drive home.

21
FIRST NEW DAY OF SCHOOL

I let Cody move at his own speed. No expectations. If he was going to need more time and be an hour late to school, so be it. To my surprise, he was up and ready on time. I drove him to school because, one, we were down a car, and two, I wasn't comfortable having him drive alone yet. He didn't even question me driving him, I think he knew what I was thinking. I dropped him off at the front entrance, wished him good luck and headed to work. We had already set a plan for the day. He could text or call if he needed to come home or just talk. He had established a support system at school and knew who he could reach out to for help. Wade, his counselor, the teachers and his friends were all prepared and ready.

My phone never left my sight all day, and I struggled to focus on much else besides how he was doing. I was ready at a moment's notice to go get him. I knew the exact way I would get there, but in the end I didn't need to go. Cody made it through the whole day. He did text me throughout the day to check in and let me know he was okay. My phone became not only my lifeline, but would also trigger fear whenever I received a phone call or text from the kids. My stomach would drop, and I would have instant anxiety: sweaty palms, rapid heart rate and everything else around me became hyper-focused on that call or text. I struggled when others called too, because it usually meant I needed to handle something that I knew

I either had no headspace for or no idea how to handle. I was in a constant state of low-level anxiety. This has taken a long time to fade, and I still feel a pinch of fear every now and then, but now I pause and set my mind right before I answer.

Cody made it to school the rest of that week and all the way until the end of the school year. There were rough days. I got one phone call from a teacher who was concerned about Cody because he was having a hard time staying awake in the morning class; I was grateful for the call because it allowed us to make a dose adjustment to his medication so he was less groggy. But we also realized that he was just plain tired from the stress and anxiety of going back to school. Each passing day did get better, but we stayed on our course of treatment. Even when Cody had school, we stuck to our same daily recovery routine. Talk, exercise, meditation, journaling if needed, and counseling twice a week. During one of our talks, he shared how everyone was treating and talking to him at school. He said the students did great and were comfortable talking, but the teachers were more apprehensive in their communication. I told him that made sense to me. It would seem the students could relate more to what he was going through, but as a teacher, they were not walking in their students' shoes. Many students opened up to Cody about their own struggles with depression and anxiety. He didn't realize how many other students were also in emotional pain.

Although Cody was adjusting well, he still had times he would struggle with his depression or other triggers. I reflected on times when Cody was younger. He was always afraid no one would come to his birthday parties or events. He had a difficult time being around a group of people where he would have to make conversation or felt like he couldn't easily leave. Back then, I didn't realize those were emotional triggers. I thought it was my job as a parent to help him overcome that. Maybe that is correct to a point, as we do need to help our children walk through fearful situations; but it's also imperative that as parents we realize what are potential triggers for our children and, when necessary, not force something.

On the day of Dana's 8th grade promotion, I noticed Cody was anxious and sleepy, and I knew he was off. We immediately sat down to talk and he shared what was going on. He just felt like he couldn't go. He knew there would be so many people there, including a bunch of parents he hadn't seen yet. He didn't feel confident in going. I completely understood and agreed. Dana of course wanted her brother there, but she would understand. I would not be being honest if I didn't say I was sad for her. Cody wanted to tell her himself, so I watched him walk upstairs to tell Dana as she was getting ready. I felt the pain both of my children were in and I couldn't fix it for them. It took me back to my own youth and the disappointments I had experienced. Mine was an alcoholic father; for Dana, it was Cody's mental illness. One thing was clear, they didn't have to question each other's love for the other. Dana and Cody would both have pain from this, but it would be something they would work through in time. At the time, none of that was as clear as it is now, but I was learning at an exhausting pace.

Dana's 8th grade promotion went as well as it could, and she was the epitome of brave. My niece Emma had come over and done Dana's hair – she looked adorable. I got pictures with Cody before we left. Dana had to be there early, so once I dropped her off, I parked and waited for my sister Marita to arrive. I didn't want to risk walking in by myself; I hadn't been around any of these other families since everything happened with Cody and I didn't feel up to making conversation. I wanted to find my seats for Will and my family who would be arriving later, hide in my sister's shadow and focus on my daughter.

When Marita arrived, I explained my plan and she was on board. I'm sure she would have agreed to anything at that moment, just to support me. We were making our way up the auditorium hallway when I grabbed her hand and pulled her to the wall right before entering the auditorium. She looked at me puzzled until she saw I was shaking. I told her I needed a minute. A wave of anxiety had come over me. Tears were flooding my eyes, my heart was racing and I was for the first time fearful that I couldn't control the anxiety I was battling. I felt like a spotlight was shining on my face exposing me to everyone there. Marita held on to my hands and talked calmly to me, letting me know I could do this, and that it was going to be okay. I focused on her voice and the words she spoke while trying to slow my breathing. I was angry; I wanted to enjoy my daughter's promotion and have a normal night. It took about five minutes for the anxiety to subside before I could start walking again. Marita stayed right by my side. We found seats and I sat down as fast as I could. Will and the rest of the family arrived and I finally felt at ease.

The ceremony was going well until one of the principals forgot to announce Dana's name as co-valedictorian. I was mentally jumping out of my chair, screaming, *Are you kidding me?!* A few other choice words were also going through my mind that I won't repeat. Thankfully, either another student or the assistant principal brought the omission to the principal's attention and she immediately apologized and acknowledged Dana. I knew Dana already felt awkward just being in front of all these people who knew what was happening in our home, let alone having more attention drawn to her. She was brave.

Our story was in the forefront of people's minds, and it was an uncomfortable time. They didn't know what to say to Dana, but when they did, she handled herself beautifully. The night ended with a celebration of Dana at home with her brother, family, presents and dessert. This was the start of a new chapter and we were excited for her.

22
I HAD TO GO –
NO ONE SHOULD HAVE FOUND YOU

I was having a particularly emotional day at work, so decided to take off early. I needed some time alone to clear my head. My negative head talk was on overdrive as I drove my 12-minute commute home. Summer was right around the corner. With that came the fact that both kids would be home and I still wasn't functioning very well. Even though they were both in sports over the summer, I knew they would also want to go and do things with their friends. This meant I wouldn't know where Cody was every minute of the day. Sounds like no big deal, right? Well, it wasn't. We knew Cody would have setbacks every now and then as he worked through the depression – you don't walk out of treatment healed.

I was on red alert at all times. I noticed I was short-tempered, and I felt that every nerve in my body was on overdrive trying not to miss anything. It felt like a constant push and pull of emotions. One day fear would win, and the next day hope; then despair would win the day even though courage had showed up to the fight. I never knew what emotions I would wake up to, nor did I know what Cody, Dana or Will's emotions held for a given day. I was weary. I needed to go for a drive all by myself, and I knew where I needed to go. I didn't want the kids to know and I didn't want Will to worry. I had mentioned my planned destination to Will earlier, but he wasn't comfortable with me going. I was stuck emotionally and trusted this would help me. I needed to go and see where I almost lost Cody. I needed to break through this wall of fear I was building as it was getting harder for me to escape.

I arrived home from work and parked in our driveway, but didn't open the garage door. I didn't want the kids to know I was home, they thought I was still at work. This was my window of time to go. I called Will and told him where I was going. He knew from the sound of my voice there was no talking me out of it. He asked that I stay in contact with him, which I understood and agreed with. Next, I had to call our friend who had picked up Cody's car that night, and ask him exactly how to get there. It can be very confusing if you don't know the area well, which I didn't. You can imagine his response on the other end of the line. He said calmly, "Angie, I get it, you need this, but this concerns me. Do you want me to meet you there?"

I could feel myself getting angry – not because of his concern, but because I had no response that would make sense to him or anyone. I understood that my friends and family were worried about me, but I knew this would help me. I needed closure. I just needed to go.

I said what I hoped would calm him, "I'm okay, I just need to do this. Will knows I'm going. I promised to check in."

"Okay, I understand," he said with hesitation.

I could tell by his voice he wasn't completely convinced, but he gave me the information I needed.

The drive was going to take about 30 minutes. I decided to have no music in the car as I wanted to work and feel through the thoughts in my mind. Burying them wasn't working; I needed to feel and face them. Tears started and continued one after another down my face. I didn't try to stop them. I was alone with my pain and could finally release the emotions that desperately wanted out of the chamber I had locked them into. I had, over many weeks, shoved them down, partly due to necessity at times and partly due to my downright fear of not being able to handle them. I felt I was on the verge of a breakdown. As I drew closer to the actual location, I felt emotional pressure rising in my chest, searching for a way out as my thoughts were overlapping each other. It was ugly. I tried to envision what it must have been like for my son to take this pain-filled drive, knowing what he was planning to do. The sorrow I felt reached the deepest part of my soul.

The roads started getting windy, which caused my thoughts to pause as I maneuvered each curve. I rounded the last corner and I saw what my friend had clearly described to me. I slowed down and pulled into the gravel area and parked. It was a clear, beautiful, sunny day. I rolled my window down and instantly felt the sun warm my skin. A slight breeze caused the trees around me to sway and I could smell the beginning of summer.

I looked around and found the area where his car must have been. My tears began to flow more heavily as I imagined the magnitude of my son's pain and agony. Guilt was tearing me apart and vials of anger began to exude out of me at a rapid pace. I literally screamed hateful things at God. *Where was the meaning in all of this? Why did this have to happen to Cody? Why didn't I see it? How do I help my son and daughter?* The whys and hows just kept coming. I tore myself down with my own words. *What if Cody doesn't get better or Dana gets depressed? I can't bear to lose them. I won't be able to handle it. I'm not strong enough. I'm not brave enough. People think I'm strong. I'm not. I've lost all my confidence. What if I say something or do something that causes them more pain? I want to help them through their pain, but I'm so fearful. I don't know all the steps I need to take. I don't have a plan. I don't know how to do this.*

I grabbed my journal and started scribbling all these words onto paper. The thoughts were coming too quickly, I couldn't write fast enough. My tears were falling on the pad and blurring my words. I felt rage as I grabbed the notepad and threw it against the car's dashboard and started screaming through hysterical tears. *I love them so much. I can't lose them.* My tears couldn't stop, my head was pounding and my eyes could barely open, but I let it all come out. I let it all escape. I let my emotions be freed and finally felt the heaviness of my soul lighten and my tears slow.

I got out of my car and walked to where I found a log and sat down among the trees in silence. I noticed my thoughts were finally quiet and the pressure in my chest was lifted. I don't know if you have seen the movie *The Green Mile*, but there is a scene in it where the main character has the ability to supernaturally remove ailments or pain from someone and dispel it out through himself like a wave of matter. That is what I felt had just happened to me – I had allowed myself to let go of a tremendous amount of pain.

As I sat on that log reflecting, a lone cyclist rode by. How poetic that moment was. *That's next,* I thought to myself. I realized I needed to find the man who saved Cody's life, and I needed to ask Cody a question that had been haunting me. I needed this answer to know how best to help him.

I became aware of the time and realized I needed to check-in like I promised. I texted Will, letting him know I was on my way back. I got back in my car to head home. As I drove away, I looked in my rearview mirror and said to myself, *It is time to put that rage in your past and move forward.*

I arrived home and walked in the door. I knew something was off. Will shared that he and Cody had a disagreement. I can't even tell you what it was about now. Normally that wouldn't be something to be completely alarmed about, but we weren't in a normal situation. Typically, I would worry that Cody might shut down; I would be afraid we were not handling the situation correctly. However, I was calm this time. After the afternoon I had, I felt more prepared to have an open conversation with Cody. Normally, this would have been one of those times that I just put my emotions on the backburner and tried to smooth things over. But I knew that wouldn't help us all in our healing journey – we needed to work through it.

I headed upstairs to talk with Cody. He was about ready to get in the shower, but I asked if we could talk for a moment. I'm sure he wanted to wait until after his shower, but he must have heard something in my voice because he said, "Okay Mom." We actually managed to resolve the disagreement issue quickly, but that wasn't the only reason I needed to talk. I needed to ask him my question, as the answer would let me know his truth and give me my direction.

I said, "Cody I need to ask you a question, and I need the real truth."

He just looked at me questioningly and said, "Okay, what is it?"

With a true sense of calm, I looked at him and asked the question that for weeks I had been too afraid of. "Do you want to live?" I was ready for whatever answer he gave. I wouldn't be able to help him, to the best of my ability, if I wasn't able to hear his truth.

"Yes, yes I do," he replied strongly.

"Okay then," I said. "I want you to know that I am committed to learning everything I can about mental illness, and I am able to hear your truth."

He smiled and lovingly said, "Thanks Mom."

He followed up with, "So can I take a shower now?"

I laughed and said, "Of course."

I walked out of the bathroom and I thought to myself how beautiful truth can be even when it is surrounded by pain. I was grateful for that talk. That fear no longer had its vice grip on me.

23

SUMMER WITH A GLASS OF ANXIETY

The school year ended with both Dana and Cody in school, which was a huge accomplishment for both of them. Summer was here, and I was grateful. We had family from Florida coming to visit, and with that came some well-deserved family outings. With each adventure or trip we took, I was celebrating that my family was together. During those times, I had to fight off thoughts of imagining Cody not being with us. It was especially difficult when I'd watch Cody and Dana together laughing and razzing each other as siblings do. Dana loved Cody, and I desperately wanted Dana to understand that he loved her too. His suicide attempt was not because he didn't love us. If it was hard for me to not shake those feelings of losing him, I assumed it was hard for Dana too. Maybe we weren't supposed to completely get over it; maybe that was what healing looked like. I didn't know or have anything to compare it with.

Cody was determined to play football, and daily doubles started in August. When he started high school his goal had been to make the varsity team all four years in three sports, but I didn't know if that was still important to him. As Cody made certain decisions, we just rolled with them. We didn't talk about any future sports plans – getting him healthy was the number one priority. We knew, from previous conversations with Cody, that he had been bullied in baseball and football, so I was cautious when he expressed his desire to play football. Even if the bullying stops, the trauma can still be there. I think people think that only smaller kids get bullied, but that's far from the truth. Cody is 6'1" tall and weighs 200lbs. Bullying happens to kids from all walks of life, shapes and sizes. It can also cause PTSD (Post-Traumatic Stress Disorder). PTSD is a mental health condition that is triggered by a terrifying event, either experienced or witnessed. Symptoms may include flashbacks, nightmares and severe anxiety, as well as uncontrollable thoughts about the event. During my research of mental health conditions, I found this one personally relatable. Not just because of the bullying, but because of what had and was happening to me and my family. I had symptoms of PTSD and it was an awful feeling.

Cody had new emotional tools he could use this football season. A new coach had been hired and I was hopeful for a better experience. The coaching staff worked with Cody to know how best to support him. They agreed to focus on open communication and clear expectations. It would be a learning experience for everyone. At the beginning of daily doubles, Cody struggled with anxiety and mood swings. He would call me and we did our best to walk through the anxiety and its possible causes. At times, I just let him talk to allow time for anxiety to pass. We focused on isolating where the fear was coming from and changing his head talk into something positive. He was interacting with his friends and being physical, which is helpful in treating anxiety. Cody wanted to work through the anxiety, even though it was very uncomfortable for him; he didn't want anxiety to be his leader. Anyone who struggles with anxiety will know that is not an easy thing to do. However, he discovered that each personal contact led him to more and more successes.

I was struggling with my own anxiety about Dana's transition to high school. It was tough enough being a little sister to an older brother in the same school, but she would be walking into a community of students who knew what had happened to her brother. I was relieved Dana was in counseling and could work through that issue along with her brother's suicide attempt. She had a lot to deal with at her young age of 14.

One evening, I got to witness one of her fears close up. It was late and I was reading in bed waiting for Cody to get home from an evening with friends, when I realized the hall light was on – I could see it shining through the bottom of my bedroom door. I got up to turn it off and noticed Dana's bedroom light was on. It was 11:30pm and she had gone to bed a couple of hours before. I quietly knocked and gently opened her door. She was wide awake working on something.

"Honey," I said in a soft voice, "why are you still up, it's late?"

She looked at me and said sweetly, "I can't go to sleep until Cody's home."

I sighed and felt the pull on my heart. I felt sadness for her.

"Oh, okay. I understand," I said, as I went and sat on the edge of her bed. I tried to reassure her that he had sent me a picture of himself with his friends earlier, which was one of our house rules. I had also just received a text that he was on his way home. She heard me and understood what I was saying, but it didn't give her what she needed to put her head down and sleep; she needed to know he was in our house before she could relax. I couldn't blame her – I was doing the exact same thing; I couldn't sleep until he was home either.

I wished I could have taken that fear away from her, but I knew this was something I couldn't fix. It would take time. I was grateful she had shared her feelings, and encouraged her to continue to talk about the things that bothered her as this would help her healing. But I wondered what other wounds were within her that she wasn't aware of yet. You can't work on a trigger that you don't know exists. I had discovered through my own healing from past traumas that you don't actually know all your triggers until they surface. Triggers don't come in a neatly wrapped package that you can unwrap at your leisure when you're feeling emotionally strong; it could be years before they rear their ugly head. They can build slowly over time or hit you completely unexpectedly. I've experienced both, and neither feels good. Sometimes, we don't want to face them. But we must attend to them if we want to get through them and become stronger. Sometimes you may need to have a verbal conversation with yourself or maybe journaling the emotions out on paper would work best for you. Talking with a good friend can also be effective, or you can seek a more professional approach with a counselor. I've used all those tools at different times in my life. It may take years for wounds to heal, but they can heal.

As the end of summer approached, Cody made another progressive step. He caught a bullpen (which means squatting behind the pitcher for long periods of time to catch the missed balls) at our home field for Carson, his friend and baseball teammate. He hadn't done anything related to baseball since his team visit. Will sent me a picture of him behind the plate catching. I broke down crying. None of us knew if he was going to play baseball again. That decision was Cody's, but that act was another healing step. His bravery and willingness to try was awe-inspiring. I wanted so badly to replace the memory of last season, but I knew I couldn't and nor could Cody. This was his journey. It's hard to let our children feel pain, but it's necessary for them to learn how to maneuver their emotions. Pain will come in life, that is guaranteed, so if we help our children by giving them better mental health tools, the better off they will be in life. Pain can give you growth and teach you wisdom.

24

THE MAN WHO SAVED CODY

*A hero is an ordinary individual who finds the strength to
persevere and endure in spite of overwhelming obstacles.*
Christopher Reeve

Summer was moving along, and I couldn't help thinking about
the man who saved Cody's life. There were still missing pieces
from that dreaded night. My brain kept trying to figure it out
on its own, but that is dangerous and wasn't working. I needed
the correct information so my brain would stop filling in the
pieces of the story. I was looking for closure on my own, and
I wasn't finding it. I needed to know what happened, and I
wanted to hear it from him.

Jenni had told me that I could reach out to him, but I didn't
know if he would be willing to tell me the details of that night.
I had no idea what that experience did to him and his family.
He had his own personal journey in all of this, and maybe it
would just be too much to relive it again, but I had to try. I had
to reach out and take the chance. He took a chance that night
when he saved Cody. He didn't know what he was walking into.
He didn't know that his act of bravery set in motion a course of
action that no one could have ever predicted. I needed to meet
and thank this man face to face. He gave my son his second
chance at life. He physically held the weight of Cody's body

and Cody's pain in his arms. He showed my son the utmost compassion and comfort that a total stranger can bestow on another human being. He saved a son, a brother, a grandson, a cousin and a friend. He will forever be my ultimate hero. I needed him to hear that from my lips.

I had his telephone number in my purse. It was speaking very loudly to me, but I was afraid of... what? I couldn't tell you. Maybe the truth would be too painful – but not knowing was creating more pain. I pulled out that little piece of paper with his name and number on it. I decided to text because I didn't know if I would be able to form a coherent sentence without falling apart. Also, if he texted back, it would allow me more time to think of my reply. I'm usually comfortable speaking on the fly, but I wasn't taking any chances on this subject.

I must have gone through ten different draft messages before I landed on something similar to this, "Hi Brock, this is Angie, Cody's mom. Your neighbor had given me your number and said it was okay to reach out. I was wondering if I could meet with you?" I read it a few more times then hit send. Then I waited. It didn't take more than five minutes before he responded. I read the text: he would like to meet me too. I was excited.

I asked if it was okay for Dana and Will to join me, but that Cody wouldn't come. Cody said he wasn't ready to see him again just yet, the emotions were too raw. Brock said he was very excited to meet all of us, and asked if his wife could be there. I said I hoped she would be. Just from those few text exchanges I felt connected to him. We set up an evening visit at his home for the forthcoming Sunday. My mind was at rest, and I had peace. I needed this conversation, and maybe he did too. I let the family know I had connected with Brock and set up our visit. Even though they were apprehensive too, they were just as excited.

Sunday night arrived quickly. Even though it was a short drive to his house, less than ten minutes, it felt like it took forever. I didn't have a plan for how the visit would go, except I didn't want to overstay our welcome. I wanted to be sensitive to Dana and watch for any clues from her that she was uncomfortable. If so, I would make an excuse to leave. We walked up a paved path to his front door and knocked. My stomach was in knots, but I also felt calm.

Brock answered the door with the biggest smile on his face. He was a fit young man, probably in his late twenties or early thirties, and around 5'10". I remember thinking to myself that he was smaller than Cody and it must have taken a lot of strength to pull him out of the car. My thoughts were racing, but I wanted to lock this memory in my head. I introduced all of us and immediately felt the need to hug him, which I did. He had the sweetest face and demeanour, such a nice man. I couldn't help but keep staring at him. I couldn't believe I was in the house of the man who saved my son. I couldn't put a name to the emotions I was feeling.

He walked us into his beautifully decorated open-plan home and introduced us to his lovely wife. He invited us to sit down in their living room – there was a couch to the right where Dana, Will and I sat; he and his wife sat in two larger chairs across from us. From the couch, we could see into his beautiful backyard, it looked into a forested green space and put you at ease.

I didn't know where to begin. My emotions were starting to surface and I could feel the tears welling up in my eyes. What do you say to someone who you know literally saved your son from death? I had never been one to think much about death, but ever since May 1st, it was part of my daily unwanted thought process. I thought to myself, *Just start talking, it will be okay.*

First, I thanked Brock for taking the time to meet with us and expressed our sincere gratitude for his heroic act of stepping in and saving Cody. He was very humble and visibly emotional as he listened to me talk. He nodded his head and smiled to let me know he was listening. He waited patiently until I was done talking and acknowledged what I said. Then, immediately, he asked how Cody was doing. I spent a good amount of time bringing him up to speed on Cody's progress. He was relieved.

I then asked him if he would be comfortable walking us through what happened that night. He shared that he had actually journaled the event. It had been a life-changing experience for him, and he felt he would never be the same. His statement was clear and strong: *A miracle happened that night.* I didn't disagree.

He continued with his part of the story. It was a beautiful day and he, his wife and her father were planning to go on a bike ride. They ended up getting a later start than they had planned. During the ride, his wife was staying close to her father. For some reason, he was having a hard time during the ride, and wanted to turn around to ride home early, which I guess was unusual. Brock said he would ride ahead, then wait for them or backtrack to where they were, and start riding again. It was during one of these backtracks that he noticed a car parked and hidden within some tall grass off the road. Something caught his eye and looked out of place. He looked again and noticed more about the scene – he saw the hose.

Brock's wife and her father soon came speeding along on their road bikes. Brock tried to draw their attention to the car, but they couldn't hear him and continued riding quickly onward, back to their cars.

Brock decided to ride over to Cody's parked car. As he got closer he realized the car was running. *This is happening right now!*, Brock thought. At that point he said his instincts kicked in. He jumped off his bike, threw it down on the gravel and ran toward the car. He said his thoughts were racing in split-second moments of thought processing. Brock considered how he would react if the person in the reclined front seat would be angry to see someone show up, and possibly be holding a gun. He ignored that possibility, and continued on his path. He reached the car's window and forcefully ripped the hose out of the cracked driver window.

He saw Cody reclined in his seat and dressed in his baseball uniform, with a handwritten note positioned on the steering wheel. He needed to open the door, but it was locked! He pounded on the window! Miraculously, Cody had just enough consciousness left to reach up and unlock the door. Brock opened the door, turned off the car and threw Cody's keys into the distance.

Brock described the precise moment of lifting Cody up in order to drag him out of the car as something unforgettable – like divine intervention. Once out of the car, he looked around and found a rock for them to lean up against. Then, he just held Cody in his arms.

He started to describe the next part of the story, but had to pause. He was looking down at the floor and I could tell he was trying to gain composure. He looked up and I could see the tears in his eyes, and his voice began to crack as he continued.

Brock said Cody was crying and kept repeating the words "thank you", and saying that he needed help. Tears were cascading down my face onto my shirt as I listened to him describe Cody's pain. It was almost too much for me to hear. The heaviness in my chest felt as if my heart was breaking, but I couldn't take my eyes off of him. He said he held Cody and told him he was going to be okay. Brock described how he was emotionally overwhelmed at that moment, realizing that he was meant to be there, at that exact time. He had no doubt it was a miracle.

Eventually, Brock heard a car approaching and was able to wave it down for help. His phone didn't have service, otherwise, he would have already called. In that car was the attendance secretary for Cody's high school. She was distraught as she told him that she knew Cody and that he was a good boy. Amazingly her phone had service; 911 was called and a sheriff arrived along with the fire service and EMTs.

Brock said the hardest part was watching the sheriff ask questions of Cody as to why he was trying to take his life, such as had Cody done something that would cause him to want to take his life. Brock said it felt harsh at the time, but on reflection he understood why the sheriff had to ask those questions of Cody. It didn't take long before the sheriff realized that he didn't need to continue this line of questioning, and his tone and actions with Cody changed. Brock finished talking and we all took a much-needed emotional break.

My guilt was staggering as I sat there in a stranger's house listening to the man who saved my son's life. Hearing him describe how he couldn't ignore the situation that he saw in front of him, and that he felt impelled to act was powerful. He described it as spiritual in nature. He said it has forever changed his life.

The emotions surging through my body felt like a wave crashing over and over on the sand with no reprieve. The pressure in my chest was back, even though I knew Cody was safe at my neighbor's house. I felt the trauma all over again. I couldn't take in all the information I was being given.

I made sure to look directly into Brock's eyes, and expressed through my wavering voice my boundless gratitude for him. I let him know that he will forever be our hero. That may sound clichéd, but it was the first time in my life that I had witnessed such heroism and a true miracle. Brock smiled back at me in a way that warmed my heart. I knew I would always be connected to him in spirit. I shared with Brock how Cody had a desire to help others like himself; he didn't know what that looked like yet, but it was a priority.

Brock asked if we could keep him updated on Cody's progress, as long as we felt comfortable doing so. I told him it would be our pleasure. He was delighted. He mentioned that he had his journal notes of that night and at some point in the future he would like to send those to Cody when he felt he was ready. I told him I'd let Cody know.

I stood up to leave, knowing it was time to go. I was beyond grateful to have gained more knowledge of what happened that night, more than I could have ever hoped to get. They walked us to the door, hugs were exchanged, and we all agreed to see each other again someday. As we walked out to our car, I was confident we all were in a better place than when we started. Our hearts were full, despite the agony and difficulty of hearing the story – we all focused on the actual, positive outcome.

I still send Brock information about Cody and how he is doing to this day. He will forever be part of our family, and forever my hero.

25

SENIOR AND FRESHMAN YEAR

The first week of the new school year coincided with Cody's 18th birthday and Dana's first day of high school. I was happy Cody and Dana had one year of high school together. I had had the same experience with my own brother; he had watched out for me and I knew Cody would do the same for Dana.

Cody's birthday this year felt different from others, on account of realizing what could have been. I was grateful and more appreciative of life. But the flip side of those emotions is that I got whispers in my ear of, *Be careful with your emotions, don't be so joyful. That's risky, protect yourself.* Fear is the stealer of joy, it can hold you captive. It was a constant struggle for me to silence those thoughts and see hope growing stronger.

Cody had "late arrival", which meant he didn't have to attend the first class of the day, so he wouldn't be taking Dana to school during the year. I was secretly glad because I wanted that car time with her. So much can be learned during that drive to and from school. We had bought Cody a used blue Ford Focus over the summer after his old car was sold. The kids nicknamed it The Blueberry after the TV show *Syke*. It felt good to move on in a positive way regarding the car. Both kids had their practice after school: Dana with volleyball and Cody with football. That part of life seemed normal, but I was personally struggling with anxiety more than ever before.

If my cellphone or home phone rang when my kids were not with me, I'd have a sense of dread. If I didn't hear Cody stir in the morning, I would get anxious. If Cody was delayed in responding to a text, I'd worry. I didn't want to go very far from home in case something happened and I needed to get to either of my children. I knew these were symptoms of PTSD, and they weren't getting better so I needed to find a counselor for myself in the near future. I wanted to get the kids transitioned first and then I made a promise to myself to get help.

Dana liked the structure of high school and her classes. She wanted to do well and enjoyed the schoolwork. She had been a competitive gymnast for a number of years, so she understood what hard work means, and it was no surprise to me that she would succeed in classes and with schoolwork. It was the social part that was harder for her. She did her best to engage in the social activities of high school, but as I reflect on this time in Dana's life, I wish I hadn't been so protective of her time and our privacy. I was overprotective. We didn't venture out as much during this time and I regret that. I think it was detrimental for Dana; what I thought I was doing to protect my family may have made it harder for her to put herself out there. This is yet another painful lesson of maneuvering through this healing process that I have had to work through and learn to forgive myself for.

Cody was doing well in football, not because of wins or losses but because of the changes in his personality. He was freer, having fun and no bullying was happening. He communicated his feelings openly to teammates and coaches, and had a healthier perspective about expectations. I could see it in him, it was like a weight had been taken off his shoulders.

One morning toward the end of fall and the beginning of winter, Cody shared with me a paper he had written late one night about the pressures of being an athlete. He said it took him just 20 minutes to write as the words flowed out of him. He felt this story might help other students who could be struggling mentally and emotionally; it might help them know they are not alone, especially as it was coming from someone who really understood what they might be going through. He also thought the story could help coaches to know what it's like from the athlete's perspective. He decided to email the story to Wade for his advice on how best to accomplish his mission to get it into the right hands. Cody trusted Wade to use it as he saw fit. Wade was so moved by the piece that he shared it with his coaching staff at their next meeting. Wade would often say how clearly different Cody was now – his walls were down; this paper was another example of the freedom Cody was displaying.

I shared his story with my sister, Marita, who ended up sharing it with her daughter's high school Athletic Director, who in turn shared it with their coaching staff. It was apparent that Cody had the ability to share a life experience in words that could move people. The feedback was humbling – coaches were emotional; it caused them to pause and take note. One person wrote, "I'm going to use this as our coaching focus for all our sports, all levels. Care and concern for our athletes above all else." Another coach sent an email that said, "This is the best and most heartbreaking thing I've ever read. I am a coach who has an impact on these kids. This matters to me."

Marita said it so well, "This story can be an eye-opener to everyone, not just coaches, but also parents, teachers, friends, that the human spirit can be more fragile than we see on the outside."

Here is Cody's paper:

I am a high school athlete. I go to a normal school. I play on normal sports teams. I am a freshman. A sophomore. A junior. A senior. I am a starter. A backup. A varsity player. A bench-warmer. I play as well as I can. I am a vocal leader who takes charge of my team. I am in the back of the group, and am afraid to even speak. I am a teammate. A player. A friend. A student. Or someone rarely heard of. I am someone who walks proudly in the halls. And someone who hides behind my own smile. I am an athlete that falls through the cracks. I am a standout player. What do I lack? Self-worth, happiness, and any form of confidence.

"Pull your head out of your ass, and get to work!" my coach screams as I make one mistake. A dropped pass, missed free throw, strikeout. I know I am not the best player on the field or court, but I try my best to do my part. All I strive to do is my best, and I give as much effort as I can. I mask my face with false emotions, and try to pick myself up from a mistake I know I made, but am powerless to fix. I didn't miss the shot on purpose, even professionals make mistakes, but my coach doesn't seem to understand that. I know when I make another mistake my coach will be back in my face screaming, or telling me that I am just not good enough. Constant criticism leaves me wondering what I do right. Will coach ever be proud of me? What can I do to impress him? After a season of this, I feel worthless. I know I messed up, but I tried to fix it. A consistent wrecking ball of risen voices, disappointment, and failure breaks through what little confidence I have as I ask myself more serious questions. Why am I failing? Would it be better if I quit? Am I good at anything? What do I play for? I wish I had an answer to any one of these questions.

"I know you are the best player. You could really go somewhere. You have an exceptional amount of talent. I am telling you what I truly think." These words enter my head bearing more weight than my coach could possibly understand. "Thank you coach!" I reply with vigor and bounce off the field beaming with a smile that lasts until I realize that the starting lineup for tomorrow doesn't include my name. My head fills with doubts as I recall yesterday's conversation with my coach. Yes, he said that I was talented. Everything he told me leads me to believe I should be out there. My mind swirls with questions as I ask my coach why I am not on the field. He tells me to relax, and to "trust the system" and that everything will work out. That he knows what he is doing. The words of reassurance ease my troubled mind and I assume the bench position.

Little do I know this will be my seat for the year, and that a week from now I will be left wondering what I did wrong, why my coach doesn't want me on the field, and how to get better. Only to be left with the same answers time and time again until my confidence is shattered, and I am left to wonder what I have to work for as an athlete.

"Holy shit man, have you always been this terrible? God, how is it that hard to kick a soccer ball. Why the hell do you even play?" My teammates belittle me as I try to make it through another day of doubles practice. I think I can handle it; I just let it go and get back to playing. My coach knows what is happening, but doesn't seem to care. Others are just oblivious to the obvious bullying on the field. Day after day, practice after practice I hear these words. Not good enough. You are shit. Get off the field faggot. I am a senior, but the words still cut deeply. When I was a freshman it was the same way. Pussy. Loser. Asswipe. I think I would've been good if I had confidence. Or my coach made it stop. I dreaded the thought of playing soccer after day one freshman year. I played because I didn't want to look like a quitter in front of them. I wanted to show them that I could take it. That they didn't affect me. I was wrong.

I do well in the classroom. I get mostly As and Bs. I can pass sometimes. I work hard to earn a C in my math class. English is even tougher this year. How am I going to balance school with sports? What if I can't pass math? Are my parents going to be mad? Will colleges even look at me? So many questions for one over-stressed mind to handle. I come to practice worried sick about my math test tomorrow, so are some of my teammates. Coach was upset because of some kid in class today, and we paid the price. Sprints from 3–4. Practice from 4–6. Extra conditioning from 6–7. Meeting after from 7–7:30. By the time I get changed, it is 8PM, and I still have a long drive home. I would love to get there, but I have to drive my friend home whose practice ends at 8:40. By the time we get home, it's 9:30. I shower and eat dinner and just want to sleep. I finally get started on my homework at 10:15, but I don't finish until 12:30. Now it is time for bed, but I can't sleep. Thoughts race about the game on Thursday, practice tomorrow, the test, my parents fighting. I don't fall asleep until 1AM and 5 hours later I'm back up for just another day of high school.

I am a high school athlete. I deal with more stress each day than most adults. I feel unwanted. Anxious. Depressed. Disappointed. Not good enough. Like a failure. I try to be strong, but sometimes I wonder how long I can handle it. I don't want to talk about how I feel because I would be seen as weak. No one knows about my struggle. No one knows I need help. No one would even miss me if I was gone. I would be better off running away, or dead. I am powerless to help myself, but I have no idea how to ask for help. I am an anonymous high school athlete, but the worst part is, you know who I am.

This story started something within Cody. Something deep was stirring and I knew more was coming, I just didn't realize what or the impact. We actually thought about making this into a video for coaches and players' training; who knows, maybe someday we will.

26
THE OTHER MOTHER

Normal life was becoming more intertwined in our recovery process. We had moved Will's dad into a new care facility. Dana had finished up her counseling and Cody was down to seeing his counselor once a week. Cody had done some college visits, and in late fall he made the decision to attend Western Oregon University. I was thrilled that he was going to be close to home. Will and I both agreed early on that we wanted the kids to experience going away to school if college was their path; I hadn't had that opportunity, but wished I could have. Cody's choice was a selfish win for me – he would be closer to home which would allow me to keep in touch with how he was doing emotionally. I was also happy for Dana because she would get to see him more and he would be able to still be part of her high school life. I didn't think about what it would be like having Cody not under my roof, and not knowing his whereabouts was something I didn't want to think about. Suicide is the second leading cause of death among college students, and that statistic scared the crap out of me.

Fear wasn't the only issue I was struggling with. I could feel myself becoming isolated. Cody, Dana and Will seemed to be moving forward, but I felt stuck. I couldn't put my finger on the exact issue. I was wrestling with anger, trust, spirituality and confidence. I noticed my behaviors and old ways of living had changed. I could no longer listen to the news; I couldn't watch certain movies; I reacted with fear when I would hear about other mental health emergencies; I stopped eating certain foods (I can't explain that one). At bedtime my routine had always been to do a crossword puzzle to help me sleep – I couldn't do that anymore. I couldn't look at pictures from before May 1st because I would analyze Cody's face to see if I could see anything that looked wrong. I can't explain it, these things just happened.

I did use music during the whole experience to help me connect on both a spiritual and emotional level. The words of songs spoke to me in a healing way that made it easier for me to cope. I would replay songs over and over. It wasn't just one genre of music, it was from all over the board. Music allowed my tears to flow and helped pain leave my body, but it was exhausting because I felt like I was repeating the same emotional highs and lows and not moving through them. It felt like I was stuck in a time warp. I used my commute to release most of my tears. It's great how sunglasses not only shield you from the sun but from other drivers. You can be having a full-blown meltdown in your car, but to other drivers you're just coasting through your day.

My extended family and friends were all there to support me, but I still felt alone. I was part of a club that none of them belonged to. I felt that for me to move forward I needed someone with similar experience to talk to. It was my time to seek help.

I wasn't ready for a formal counselor but knew that was in my future. I wanted to see if I could find someone like me. I reached out to a trusted friend for some help and guidance, and that meeting proved invaluable. He was able to connect me with another mother who had just experienced a similar situation and was open to meeting. This was hugely important for me. My family was aware I was struggling and they were glad I had found someone to talk with.

These meetings with the other mother were the most healing times during my journey. It's like Cody described when he was in treatment: he found someone like him who was struggling with depression and it helped him not feel alone.

What was wonderful during our times together was the amount we had in common with our emotional struggles and internal head talk. We could almost finish each other's sentences. It was the first time I spoke honestly about my deepest fears. And to hear those were her fears too made the anxiety in me calm. I felt so fortunate to have her in my life – it was a blessing.

We would meet once a week, and then every other week. We were healing in front of each other. The cavity where my darkest fears lived was being vacated through deep, intimate conversation and learning to forgive myself. Even though our situation details were unique, our emotions were similar – we shared a common bond. We spoke truth to each other, and through that silenced much of our negative head talk. It was the catalyst I needed to move forward and take the next step, which was to meet with a professional counselor. I felt I could now focus on deeper issues having cleared away the messiness of the other issues where I felt alone.

I would still have days where the impact of the event would slide from the back of my head to the front, but this was becoming less and less. I didn't visit the "what if" world as much, and I started to let go of the past. If fear tried to direct my steps, hope would lay a beautiful stone to send me in a better direction. There is a quote from *The Shack* by William P. Young, "Pain has a way of clipping our wings and keeping us from being able to fly. Left unresolved for a long time, you can almost forget that you were ever created to fly in the first place." I didn't want to be that bird.

I can't tell you exactly when the other mother and I stopped meeting. It happened naturally. We have stayed in touch over the years and kept tabs on our families. It's nice to know we are looking out for each other, even though we are not part of each other's daily lives. People come into our lives for a reason; I had known this mom years before in a different circle of friends. Who would have thought when we first met all those years ago that we would someday provide each other a healing hand.

27

COURAGE

Courage: The ability to do something that frightens one.
Strength in the face of pain or grief.

It was January 2014 and winter sports had started. Cody was playing racquetball and Dana was in winter track to prepare for the upcoming spring cross-country season. The other sport that does winter workouts is baseball; its goal is to help players prepare for spring tryouts. They are not mandatory, but it was something Cody participated in every year around his racquetball schedule. This winter I had no idea what Cody's plan was. Cody was being encouraged by teammates and friends to come to the baseball practices. They would either talk to him at school and or send him encouraging text messages. One teammate sent a picture of the inside of his baseball hat with the number 13 written in it, which was Cody's jersey number the previous season. It meant a lot to Cody that they were reaching out and supporting him without any pressure. No matter what his decision, Cody didn't have to wonder whether they wanted him to play. I was grateful Cody shared these moments with me because it allowed us to naturally have a conversation about baseball and walk through his feelings. Baseball was still a trigger, but I could see him trying to process how he felt and dig deeper into the actual cause of the trigger. He had been specifically working on this issue with his counselor and Wade. He felt he was making good progress. Even if he didn't end up playing, he didn't want to ignore the situation.

As a parent, I think you never know how much to encourage or push your child through emotional discomfort, fear or anxiety. The intent is to help them face and maybe even conquer their fears to help build that skill because they will face those in everyday life, but there is a delicate balance. You want them to realize that what may seem impossible *is* possible, or help them to see that the more you face issues that are uncomfortable the more comfortable they may become. I realize this doesn't work in every situation. The hope is they are able to work through the fear or anxiety and not have it hold them back or affect their quality of life. Anxiety can freeze and cripple you; it can stop you from moving forward, or from trying new things. It can take a great amount of work to get to the root cause and get to the other side. Sometimes it takes many attempts and much effort to get there. Emotions are powerful; they can empower us to do great things or destroy our confidence to try. I knew baseball was going to be a sensitive topic.

I wanted to have a deeper conversation with Cody about baseball, I just didn't know how to start the conversation, so I did what is comfortable and best for me in these types of situations. I wrote him a letter. I felt this was the best way to convey my feelings and thoughts while not breaking down into tears. The tears were not about playing baseball, they were about the sadness I had that he had lost his love of the sport and the amount of pain it caused him.

My words expressed that any decision he made, we supported – hands down, not even a question. Secretly, I feared that if he went back he could have a relapse. But I also didn't want fear to hold him back. I was concerned either way, but that was not what I needed to say. I needed to share his own story from my eyes. How, at a young age, he fell in love with baseball, from the moment he caught his first ball to learning how to bat.

He would write about baseball for school assignments, read books relating to baseball and collect baseball memorabilia. He collected baseball cards, baseball balls and anything to do with the Seattle Mariners. Our family knew of Cody's collections and would pick up baseball souvenirs during any of their travels and bring them home for him.

He hit his first home run at eight years old, along with an unassisted triple play in the same season. He hit the cycle. If you're not familiar with that baseball term, it is the accomplishment of the batter hitting a single, a double, a triple and a home run in the same game. He had played most positions on the field over the years, which gave him a deeper understanding of the strategy of baseball, but his favorite position was catcher. He loved the mental part of the offense and defense in that position. Cody could hit. It was uncanny how many times Cody was placed in situations where a base hit was needed and he delivered. I earned many grey hairs over the years.

My hope in this letter was for Cody to know why it may have hurt so much when he lost his love of baseball. It wasn't just any sport to him. I wanted him to be able to look back years later, and feel good about the decision to play or not. I shared these thoughts to help him remember why he fell in love with baseball and to encourage him to not have anyone or anything take that from him.

Whether he played ever again, I still hoped that through healing he would find his love of the sport, even if it was as a spectator. I finished the letter and put it away knowing I would give it to him when the time was right – which didn't take long.

One night before the winter baseball practices were set to start, Cody received a call from the new head baseball coach. He had been the assistant coach from last year. He had a good relationship with Cody, and his son also played for the team. The coach was calling to encourage Cody to come to winter baseball practice the following night, but with no expectations.

He then went into a more personal conversation with Cody, asking what he could do to help him. He understood it would be difficult for Cody to come to practice. He wanted Cody to have the best chance of success if he chose to come out for baseball in the spring. Cody felt his sincerity, and it mattered that he called. He told Coach he would seriously think about it, and thanked him for the call. I could see the wheels turning in Cody's head. I sat patiently, letting Cody work through the emotions he was feeling. He looked at me.

"Mom, I think I want to try and go tomorrow," he said very calmly.

I looked at him and said, "That is a courageous decision and, no matter what, it will be another healing step."

In one breath I was nervous for him, and in another excited for him. He knew he needed to make a decision and the only way to do that was to try.

The next night, I watched him grab his baseball gear like I have so many times, but this time was different. He was stepping out to bravely face the unknown. To be brave means "ready to face and endure danger or pain, showing courage." There would be no physical pain, but there would be emotional pain, and he had no idea how his body would respond but he went anyway. I gave him a hug and wished him good luck. He loaded all his baseball gear into his car and smiled at me as he backed out of our garage. I gave him a thumbs up and off he went. I was anxious but at peace. Not typically two words that go together, but I felt good because he was learning to use his new coping skills, and he looked excited.

The next two hours flew by and it felt like only moments had passed when I heard the garage door, which meant Cody was home. He walked in and said very matter of fact, "It went okay, a good okay."

He genuinely felt that everyone was glad to see him. I told him that didn't surprise me. His demeanor was relaxed, so I took a chance and told him I had written him a letter about baseball and asked if I could read it to him.

He looked at me puzzled, which he should have. Then I told him it was his story, and he looked even more confused. I kind of chuckled at his expressions.

I went upstairs and grabbed the letter from my dresser drawer. Once I got back downstairs, Cody was visibly intrigued as we sat down across from each other in our living room. I started to unfold the letter to read it, then suddenly stopped. I folded the letter back up and gave it to him. I said, "I'd rather tell you your story from my heart." I started talking and he patiently sat listening until I was finished. We both had tears in our eyes and smiles on our faces. We spent the next moments sharing baseball memories from his youth. He wished baseball now could be like it was when he was young. He recalled that then, when the game was over, he could leave all the emotions on the field and focus on what was really important – who was in charge of the Capri-Sun and snacks. We both started laughing, but in all seriousness he was right. I'm not sure when it happened, but somewhere along the way baseball lost its joy; I just hoped Cody could find it again. I told him impishly that if he decided to play that maybe Coach would let me bring the snack tradition back. We laughed again and agreed that would be a great plan.

It was an evening I will always remember. I hold that conversation as one of my most treasured from Cody's recovery. That evening I received numerous texts from parents saying how they heard Cody was at practice, and how excited their sons were to come home and tell them he was there. They wanted to share how much they admired Cody for making that courageous step. They knew Cody may not play, but they wanted me to know they also hoped he would. In my mind, I saw a good group of boys playing some ball, having fun, winning some games and making memories. I wanted the warm and fuzzy – the relationships.

The boys were changed emotionally by what had happened with Cody. Cody was changed. This could be a season of recovery for all. I felt something new was on the horizon. People were sharing their emotions and how they felt about one another. I saw it first-hand when Coach asked Cody what he could do for him. That's what sport at this level is supposed to be about. Team sports were not all about building skills and winning; team sports should also be about developing individual character, respecting your fellow teammates and building relationships through teamwork. I like to win like everyone else, but not at the expense of a person's spirit. It was about learning to win in losing and celebrating in the wins together.

Cody continued going to winter baseball practices on and off around his racquetball season. Only time would tell whether he would play in the spring. What I knew for certain was that he was healing, and he wasn't the only one.

28
MARRIAGE AND FAMILY – THE UGLY TRUTH

Anyone who knows me, understands me to be private, which is why writing this book is such a huge step of faith. I'm not going to share all of my marital ups and downs, but I'm not going to sugarcoat my marriage either. That wouldn't help anyone. I try to be a speaker of truth. My two older nieces say that I'm now Angie 2.0, because this experience has made me speak even greater truth. That's why this chapter is important for me to share. I won't be airing our dirty laundry, I don't work that way, but I will be truthful. I do this so whoever reads this knows there is pain in the recovery, but stay the course as it does get better.

I shall start off by saying I am a flawed human being and so is my husband. We are flawed parents. We have made mistakes. We have screwed up. We have let our own childhood trauma affect our parenting. Our children have not agreed with all the decisions we have made. I have lost my temper, I have asked for forgiveness, and I have accepted apologies. I have cried with my children. Being a parent is hard work in the best of circumstances. So you can imagine how any trauma would cause a ripple effect of enlarged emotions, bad decisions and hurt feelings.

Cody and Dana know how much they are loved. We tell them all the time. They know they are our priority.

It was rough for Will and me. Our counselors were clear with us: a suicide or suicide attempt of a child can tear a marriage apart. Why? Because each partner is in a different place as they go through their own individual traumatic response to the experience. This makes it hard to focus on working through family trauma, let alone the marriage. They are barely able to find time to address their own pain, let alone help the partner with theirs. That can lead to destructive behavior. Just because you're together doesn't mean that you will feel the same things. I guarantee you, we were not feeling the same things, which was an even bigger reason for us to be in counseling. It was hard to not be on the same page. Many times we were in completely different chapters of the healing process.

The one area we agreed on from the very first counseling session was that we would not let this destroy our family. We knew we were in the fight of our life and we had responsibility to do everything we possibly could to keep our marriage from falling apart. We both loved our children and our family, even if it meant we didn't like each other at times – which we didn't. Anyone who has been married for a long time will say it takes a village to stay married. That is not an understatement. We had friends and family who we trusted and could safely talk to or, in some situations, scream with. They were not afraid to speak the truth to us, even if we didn't want to hear it. They provided us with a fresh perspective and filled our tank with emotional support. These marital challenges made it difficult and at times impossible to parent.

My recovery looked much different than Will's. I was moving much slower – at a sloth-like pace to be exact. I struggled with having the kids out of my sight and he was trying to find time for us to connect, but I wasn't comfortable leaving the kids alone. That was an area of contention, along with many others. We couldn't embrace each other's struggles, because we were just trying to find our individual way of processing the trauma – but it was rough.

Will and I received some unanticipated help during a local running event in late summer following Cody's attempt. It was the first time I had run in a public event in a long time. Usually by this time in the year I would have already run five or six events.

It had taken me over a month to start running again after May 1st. When I did, I would often run by myself through a wilderness area close to my work. I found that I could break down and sob without having to worry someone would see me. It was my time to release negative emotions and gain endorphins, which I desperately needed. So stepping out in public and doing this local event was a big step for me.

It was during this race that Will and I ran into an old friend who knew about Cody and who asked a specific question. He asked how Will and I were doing. It took me a few seconds and a few back and forth glances from me to Will and to our friend before I decided to be honest. I told him I felt stuck, but Will was recovering faster. The friend then looked directly at Will and told him the story of a mother who was a close friend of his and had experienced a similar situation to ours. He shared that the mother was still struggling and she was two years past the event. That mother had told him how she and her husband had a different relationship with guilt and, for that reason, she was moving slower through the healing. That story had a huge impact on Will because guilt was the emotion I constantly brought up during our private conversations as the one that I was struggling with. It was a turning point for us. It was also a reminder that if we hadn't been honest with that friend we would have missed the opportunity to hear that story. Recovery steps can come in unlikely places.

It wasn't that Will didn't feel guilt, but we realized guilt meant something different to each of us. His guilt was more centered around not being available to us. When he went to work every day, he'd worry about things at home. He knew he needed to work, but wanted to be at home too. He was experiencing guilt about not being available and helping out enough; he felt he wasn't having enough interactions with the kids. My guilt was different. It was deeply entrenched in my soul. I felt I had let my children down. *How did I not see it? Maybe if I did this or did that, it would have never happened. If I had been a better mother and not missed a sign.* I knew the amount of pressure I was putting on myself was unhealthy, but it was extremely difficult to change my head talk.

As Will was dealing with guilt and stress from working, I was dealing with the stress of the day to day and the guilt of feeling I wasn't doing enough. We were both exhausted. We didn't do a good job of making time to reconnect and truly listen to each other's struggles.

We didn't always agree on how to handle the multiple situations that we were facing on a daily basis. We were both concerned that the kids would see the difficulty between us, and we didn't want them to think it had anything to do with them. That was our greatest fear. These were our issues as a couple that we needed to work through. We were trying, but it was hard. I was withdrawing and Will couldn't figure out how to help me, and I couldn't tell him what I needed because I didn't know. I tried to calm his fears about him being at work, but he just felt helpless. We were not speaking each other's emotional language.

Well, guess what? And I'm sure this won't be a surprise – the kids knew we were struggling. We ended up having an honest conversation, and what they just needed to hear from us was that we were working on it and trying to make it better. They didn't need details, and we weren't planning to share those anyway. We told them we were committed to making things better, and that itself gave them the peace they needed. We all agreed to keep the lines of communication open and to be patient with each other as we were all healing.

Will and I fought hard for our marriage. It took time, years actually, but we made it. We would not always be on the same page, but we were at least finally in the same chapter and on the same team. We learned, through continuous talking and tears, to fight for each other instead of fighting against one another. We learned how to give each other distance when needed. We lowered our expectations. We listened to our counselors. We worked on our communications. Tears, so many tears. Angry and sometimes screaming conversations. The screaming came from me. I just had so much pain I needed to get out. There were a few silent treatments, but we dug our heels in and got our emotions dirty. It was ugly at times, and hard on the kids. We didn't always treat each other well in front of them, but I couldn't protect them from everything. They also saw something beautiful in the mess – we were making it. We might have looked beat up, but we were not broken. We were healing and giving each other grace. We began to make new memories and trust each other again. Our emotions were wounded but healing. I could see the finish line. It had been a marathon, but we became better people, spouses and parents for it.

29

AN ADVOCATE IS BORN

As Cody was working through the process of baseball at each winter practice, a new desire was rising within him. He wanted to share his story with other students – he thought he could help them. It took me back to the night in the ER when he asked Will and me to help him not have what happened to him happen to any other teenager. I'm sure Cody didn't even know what he exactly meant at the time, except it was in his heart. I could see it coming more into focus as I listened to him. He wanted to talk to his health teacher and see if she would allow him to tell his story and start educating students on mental health. He didn't want other students to feel alone in their struggles.

I thought back to how Wade shared how so many students reached out for help after hearing what happened with Cody. Cody thought it would be helpful for them to hear his experience and message of hope. I couldn't have agreed more. I suggested he talk to his counselor and Wade to get more direction. He said he had actually already talked to them both and they had provided some suggestions and protocols for doing a presentation. He now needed to talk to his health teacher to get something started. I was excited for him, but also hesitant as he would be putting himself out there with a new set of unknowns. I expressed my concerns, and he said that the counselor was specifically working with him on his boundaries and how he would handle the student interactions. I didn't want Cody feeling responsible for students who may share their personal information with him. Once Cody told me he and his counselor were working together, I felt better. I was on board with this idea and proud of him. He wanted to make a difference. He had no idea how that step would turn into a beautiful path, and that path would lead to a bridge that took his personal experience of depression and suicide into the world of mental health awareness.

Cody worked with his very excited health teacher and, with the approval of administration, it was a go. Cody worked hard on the presentation. During this same time, he was winding up his counseling. He had been going for nine months, and what a transformation there had been. His last day was bittersweet. I had the privilege of sitting in for the last 15 minutes. It was a time of celebration, laughter and reflection. And it wasn't "goodbye", it was "so long". Cody knew if he needed a tune up or faced something he needed help with at any point, his counselor would be a phone call away. They had a bond; we all did. From that first phone call I made sitting on the deck, where I could barely speak a comprehensible sentence, to relaxing in his office and honoring Cody's hard work and dedication to the process. I want to extend a huge thank you to all the mental health professionals who help us maneuver our way through our mental health crises. Each of our counselors was instrumental. We were all making steady progress, even if there were a few derailments along the way. No clock or calendar is required for a healing process.

The following month Cody spoke to the freshman health class. It was well received. His health teacher gave him some great feedback for future presentations – they both agreed that more time was needed. Cody could have easily talked longer, but the class time was all they had. They didn't get to finish the Q&A and the students wanted to keep going even after the bell rang to change classes. They related to Cody and his story. He was one of them. A peer. He was speaking their language. He was living their life. I asked Cody if he was nervous and he said, "Only in a good way." Cody and I were both sensitive to Dana after the presentation, knowing that some of her peers who may have not known about Cody, definitely knew now. I tried my best to keep her talking, asking her what made her uncomfortable so we could try not to put her in harm's way. She supported Cody and did her best to bend and adapt to situations around us. She was, and still is, a resilient young woman.

I don't talk a lot about Dana's struggles because those are hers to share, not mine, but it was difficult for her and she would say fear was her biggest struggle. She was able to take what she learned in counseling and talk with Cody about her fears. I can share one situation that I believe is important that they worked through.

I accidentally walked in on them talking upstairs in Cody's room. They were sitting on the edge of his bed. He had his arm wrapped round her shoulder and her head was against him. She was crying. I realized what was happening and slowly exited the room.

Later she shared with me that she had asked Cody how he was doing and he had looked at her and said he was okay, but had then asked how she was doing. That was all it took for Dana to break down crying, which gave her the courage to face her fear with Cody. She was afraid that he would try to take his life again. He encouraged her by having her focus on how far he had come. It would have been a difficult conversation for both of them, but for Dana it must have been terrifying to talk with Cody. She was brave and faced her fear, which was part of her healing process. It also allowed Cody to be sensitive to that area in Dana. She was relieved after she talked with Cody. Her journey of healing was as (and, at times, more) important as Cody's. I believe siblings try hard not to rock the boat or do anything to add to the current mix of chaos. This can cause them to withdraw or push down emotions.

Dana climbed and conquered a huge mountain of fear by sharing her emotions with her brother. Her healing gained momentum that day. She would still have fear, but it would no longer have the same power over her. The more we talk openly with family and friends about mental health struggles, the better off we all can be.

30

A NEW NUMBER FOR A NEW SEASON

Spring was upon us, which meant baseball season was soon to follow. Cody still hadn't made a decision, but the practices over winter went well. He did want Will and me to attend the parent meeting for baseball to keep his options open. We would follow Cody's lead in regards to anything related to baseball; this had to be his decision.

The meeting took place in the high school cafeteria. We knew we would be a little late because of Will's work schedule, but I hadn't thought anything of it until we arrived and 90% of the parents and players were already there. I was extremely uncomfortable walking in so conspicuously. It's on those occasions that my mind goes into overdrive and assumes people's thoughts: "Is Cody going to play?", "I wonder how the family is doing, it must be so hard?" – normal thoughts that anyone would think, yet it didn't stop the lump in my throat from growing. I wished at that moment to be able to hide behind anything or anyone. We took our seats and waited for Coach to start the meeting.

Coach discussed the new tryout process and details for the spring trip baseball tournament in Arizona. As Coach talked, I became excited, as I saw this as a fresh start for Cody. The process was clear. No position spots were given from last year. Each player had to try out for their positions. In baseball there are only nine spots on the field, which makes it extremely competitive. I have found baseball, out of all other sports, to be the most political, and the emotions of the players and parents run high.

For Cody and sports, it works best when you lay out the expectations and then walk the talk. He could handle not earning the spot he wanted, if he understood the why. And then he can move forward and focus on other ways of contributing to the team. After the meeting, Cody felt confident and good about his decision to go out for baseball. It was clear he was doing it for all the right reasons. He was different. His spirit was lighthearted. He was having fun again.

After tryout week, Cody got the call that he had earned the starting catcher spot. He was playing baseball! What that also meant was that I needed to keep my end of our agreement – I would need to clear with the Coach about bringing treats after the games. Cody and I had a good laugh about it. I was excited that he was excited about playing.

For a good two weeks after each practice, I was prepared for Cody to come home and say it wasn't working, that he had decided he couldn't play. But that day never came. He talked openly with his coaches about how he was feeling and, when appropriate, gave suggestions and feedback regarding effective ways to communicate with the players. He was speaking his truth, respectfully. The coaching staff shared numerous times with me what a difference those conversations made in their overall coaching. They too were learning new tools and perspectives. This team was special and I knew it. I was teased quite often because I saw the team through rose-colored glasses, but I didn't care, I felt it in my heart – this team was special, something momentous was happening.

Baseball is a superstitious sport, so you can imagine what we thought when Cody informed us he was no longer number 13. That had been his number in football and baseball through high school; this was a fresh start – I liked it. Deuces it was – 22.

After Cody decided to play baseball, we agreed as a family that baseball wouldn't rule our life. We agreed to spend time after each game reliving moments and talking through the win or loss, but then the game was to be put to bed, just like the field.

This team was bonding beyond baseball. A number of us parents worked with Coach to get permission to organize weekly team dinners – it's great for team building and having personal interaction outside the field. Having players in your house to share a meal and witness their interactions with each other creates fond memories. There was soul to this team. It's as if they all went back to the basics of loving the game and being grateful to be playing together. Was it perfect? No, it's sports, but it was exciting to watch the changes.

On March 17th, 2014, Sandy played our first non-league game against Estacada. This would be the first time I would see Cody play since that night almost ten months ago when everything happened. No one emotion prevailed within me – they ranged from fearful anxiety to joyfulness. I felt like a chameleon who couldn't decide which skin to wear. Cautiously optimistic became my way of explaining how I felt. My goal was to live in the moment and get out of my head, which I was thankfully able to accomplish that night.

As I walked to the bleachers through the grass, I could smell baseball. The fresh scent of mowed grass and damp wood bleachers. The sweet aroma of popcorn drifting through the chilled air. This was a second chance, a gift. I would not waste it on fear or anxiety. It was a new beginning and one to celebrate. I zipped up my jacket, put on my wool hat and headed to the snack shack. I wanted some of that popcorn. It was going to be a good night.

Cody looked relaxed behind the plate and when at bat. It was nice to see him laughing with the other players, while also taking the game seriously. The game ended in a 5-5 tie in 10 innings because of darkness, but for our family it was a homerun. Now we prepared for the spring break baseball trip in Arizona.

Before we left for Arizona, we received some disappointing news regarding Dana. She had been learning pole vault in track when she complained of back pain. At first we thought it was muscular, then I looked at her back – I took my finger down her spine and noticed it was crooked. She winced in pain when I touched the area that curved. We saw a specialist who diagnosed her with scoliosis, with a 32-degree curve and spinal rotation. During the last year she had grown almost four inches, which had aggravated the issue. Fortunately, it didn't require surgery; unfortunately, she would need to manage the discomfort until her body settled.

A week later, after a couple more non-league games, we were headed to Arizona. This was to be a family affair – we hadn't all been on an airplane since the kids were little, and this was a much overdue vacation. Dana was looking forward to the warmth and sunshine, which we were told would be good for her back. Cody would fly with us, but be with the team for the remainder of the trip until we flew home. We rented a house with Jenni and her family, which turned into a story in and of itself. We got one doozy of a house, and ended up at a Walmart buying sheets, towels, pillows, cleaning supplies and blankets. You can use your imagination as to the state of the house based on all the products we bought, but we made the best of it. We were there to watch baseball and be outside. Fortunately, the house had a great pool for Dana and the other couple's daughters, who had all grown up together.

The team didn't have a great tournament in Arizona, but that isn't always a negative; it showed where the team needed work. On the flight back home I shared with Cody that Coach was going to allow me to bring treats, but only after home games. He was shocked and actually so was I. I had to keep my promise. I didn't care what others thought. Win or lose at home, there would be treats.

31

A YEAR AGO AND BASEBALL

Life is the hardest thing you'll ever do, but it's worth it.
Cody Welty

The Sandy Pioneers baseball team started off the regular season with a one win one loss series with St Helens. Now they were headed into a two-game series against our nemesis, Sherwood, who were the defending State Champions from last year. Sherwood had a strong program and would be considered the best team in our conference. On a good day, with no errors, we could compete. Sherwood didn't make many mistakes and knew how to capitalize when other teams did. They could get in your head. We lost both games. First game 2-9 and second game 0-6.

The treats, however, were a hit; nothing fancy, just mini candy bars. After a home game was over and the Coach had finished his team meeting, I'd hand the treats over to Cody, who handed them to the boys. The players didn't know what was happening early on, but as the season continued, they looked forward to that little piece of childhood in that candy bar.

Our next two-game series was against Liberty, another strong program. We were behind by four in the first inning. In high school there are seven innings of play. By the bottom of inning five we were down 3-7. The pressure was on. Liberty's pitcher started to struggle and Sandy's bats woke up. We gained five runs that inning and tied the game. Sandy secured a one run lead by the bottom of the seventh. Coach sent in Carson, our number one pitcher, to close out the seventh inning and gave us the win. Sandy closed out the second game of the series with a 3-2 win, again coming from behind. Cody was quoted in the paper saying how comeback wins feel so much better, and how his team stayed positive even when behind. Coach also mentioned how this team competes no matter what the score is. Cody personally had a great second game, as he went 4-for-4 with a double, three RBIs (run batted in) and three runs. What moved me was the way Cody was playing: he was relaxed and free, like when he was young.

Rex Putnam was up next, with Sandy taking the sweep of three games. A total of 22 runs were scored between game two and three. Sandy's batting statistics were blazing that series – Cody ended up with a multi-hit game. That moved us into a second place tie with Wilsonville. We entered the week ranked 13 in the Class 5A hierarchy.

Relationships grew deeper over team dinners, and the spring break losses seemed a distant memory. The boys were turning a corner, not because of lucky plays or having a stand-out player hitting home runs, but because of something you can't see. If you looked at our team on paper, it didn't shout All Stars. It showed a group of boys that played together over many seasons and had the right attitude. I have never been part of a baseball team that didn't have drama, coaching issues, politics or parents overstepping their mark. This season they were playing for each other, not for themselves. There was great talent on our team, but it was spread out among the players and they trusted each other.

Over the next week, April would come to an end and May would arrive. May 1st would be a year, to the day, since Cody had attempted to take his own life.

So, how do you handle anniversaries like this? It sure as hell isn't a memory I want to relive every year. I celebrate every day that we didn't lose Cody. However, I knew that we couldn't ignore the day. So, what do you do? In our situation, Cody made it clear. He had mentioned many times in treatment and since that he viewed May 2nd as a new beginning or birth – a second birthday per se. So we decided that May 2nd would become the anniversary to celebrate. Cody had actually written "Day 1 of Ass Kicking" in the May 2nd square on our refrigerator calendar when he first got home from treatment.

That first of May, I took the time to give thanks that he was saved. I never want to take that miracle for granted. I reflected and gave thanks and read through my journals to remind me of the distance we had traveled. Our healing journey wasn't over, it's a process, but I was celebrating a year that had been filled with hope.

The final game of the series against Milwaukie fell on May 2nd. We agreed to celebrate after the game with ice cream. Sandy ended up crushing Milwaukie 14-2 in game three to again earn a sweep. Cody almost got his first home run of the season – he hit a curveball to the gap in left-center and that one hopped the fence. This team was hitting well, playing solid defense and being aggressive on base running; round that out with strong pitching, and this team was fun to watch as they earned their eighth win in a row.

Now it was time to celebrate. Dana rode with Cody as we headed to get ice cream and then home for him to open his present. This worked for our family, and still does to this day. If we can't all physically be together, we take time to Skype and a gift reaches Cody wherever he is.

I want to express the strangeness of the emotions I felt on that first anniversary. The year before, after his game, I had received a call informing me that my son attempted to take his life. One year on, after his game, I was celebrating his continued recovery. Through the previous 12 months I had had no idea where we'd be that day. I had only been able to make one thought, one decision, one step at a time. I had questioned decisions constantly. I would talk to myself out loud to bring clarity to my own thoughts. It was a dark time.

If you are in this darkness right now, I want to encourage you. The steps never seem to be straight and that's okay. Each story is unique and the movement to recovery can be difficult. But don't give up, consider switching the direction of treatment. Be bold, fight for your or your loved ones' mental health, even if it means you need to be more direct with the professionals you're working with. Perhaps try a new doctor, get guidance on changing medication, try a different counselor or, when necessary, call that emergency number if you are in crisis. Keep searching for the right combination, and hold on to hope.

32

SECRETS

Cody was approached by an English teacher at Centennial High School, Nicole, who was the daughter of one of my co-workers. Nicole taught a narrative writing unit called "Secrets" that engaged with social emotional learning. Given that narrative writing is steeped in personal experience, the unit provided students an opportunity to anonymously share their stories by writing down their secrets on notecards, from which they would then develop writing skills around those personal experiences. What Nicole had learned was that the unit not only provided students with technical learning, but had become a safe community for students to share similar secrets in, as well as a form of cathartic healing for a number of kids.

The students' secrets were raw, honest and deeply personal, often centering around suicidal ideation and their inner struggles. The theme of the unit was inspired by author Frank Warren, whose ongoing community mail art project, "PostSecret", addresses the same concept: sharing secrets anonymously as a way to connect and offer a voice and healing to those who need it. Nicole had learned there was power in students hearing the stories of their peers, and realized she needed to take the social emotional learning to the next level by bringing in a guest speaker.

Nicole was aware that Cody had spoken to the Health class at his high school and wanted to know if Cody would be interested in sharing his story again with her two English classes. She felt strongly that his real-life story would speak to her students. Cody and Nicole met up for coffee, and from there they worked on a plan that would pair Cody's story with her class assignment.

Cody knew he had to address this group of students slightly differently to how he had spoken to the Health class at his school because these students didn't know anything about him. He would need to add a personalized layer to connect with these students. He was able to finalize his presentation in the midst of baseball defeats against Parkrose and schoolwork. He decided that, since these students were older, like himself, he could discuss in more detail the emotional and mental health struggles he was dealing with, thus providing more education on his recovery process. He would still maintain his focus on hope and recovery, but provide more personal details. He was to make his presentation on the Monday following Senior Night (the last regular home game of the season).

33

CELEBRATING IN LOSS

During the last week of regular season home games, it became clear that Will's dad, Dennis, who had been slowly deteriorating over the last year, was not going to make it through the week. On Monday we went to say goodbye to him. We had never told Dennis what had happened with Cody – it was unnecessary in his condition. When we got to his care home, he was sleeping peacefully. We didn't know if he could hear us, but we sat round his bed and reminisced with stories about Grandpa. Laughter filled his room and, when it was time to go, each one of us said our personal goodbyes. Tears welled up in all of us as we left Dennis for the final time and walked to our car. Dennis had lived a good life, but it felt too soon. Will and I had both lost a parent earlier in our relationship; my dad died when I was 22 and had just graduated from college, and Will lost his mom to cancer when he was just 24. This was especially hard for Will, knowing that both his parents were going to be gone. Will was adopted, and had had the opportunity to meet and develop a relationship with his birth mother, but the parents who had raised him were going to be gone.

That Friday was the last home game against Wilsonville, and it was also Senior Night. A group of us parents worked to get baseball pictures of each of the seniors from when they were small. We enlarged the photos, glued them to a poster board and tied them to the baseball fence. A couple of weeks before, my niece Alyssa, who is a photographer, had come out and done a photo shoot with the Seniors. They were a bunch of goofballs during the shoot, but we got what was needed.

Before the game, each Senior walked out onto the field with their family and a few words were spoken about their plans for after high school. It was a night of recognition. After the ceremony, it was time to play ball.

It was a tight game. It was the bottom of the seventh and we were down 5-3. We needed two runs to tie and three to win. Sandy had a stressful habit of coming from behind to win a game. Our fan base had been growing throughout the season, but that night the crowd was especially large because of Senior Night. The team did their magic. We gained two runs with a single, walk and sacrifice bunt that moved the runners around the bases. Then our lead-off batter laced a base hit to left center and two runs scored. The crowd was on its feet roaring. I couldn't believe what I was seeing. We were now in a tie game with our winning run on third. If you watch baseball long enough, you can start to predict when your kid is going to be at bat, based on what is happening in the game. I had a sinking feeling about what was coming. Our next batter walked and now Cody was up to bat. An acid feeling was building in my stomach. I wanted this so much for him and the team. I wanted to erase last season and all the pain it brought. I was grateful for the crowd noise as it drowned out my thoughts. Cody seemed calm as he made his way to the plate. On a 1-2 pitch, Cody hit a chopper between first and second base, but the second baseman was too deep to get a good throw home. The Sandy Pioneers won by his walk-off hit! The crowd went wild, screaming as the team raced out of the dugout and piled on top of Cody. I started jumping up and down as tears of joy filled my eyes.

Will immediately called his sister, who was with Dennis, to let him know the outcome of the game. As his sister told Dennis about Cody, he smiled. Will hung up the phone only to have his sister call a few minutes later to say their dad had passed. In that moment of celebration, heaven received a wonderful man who had loved his family. We knew he would have been so excited for the win, but also for the upcoming play-in game. I missed him already. I decided that for each game we got to play, I would bring Dennis's walking cane as good luck because over the years Grandpa had used his cane to express his happiness and frustration at the kids' sporting events. That cane could make a lot of bleacher noise. I wiped away my tears and blew a kiss up to heaven. He would be so proud of this team and their 13-game winning streak to close out the regular season.

Coach would say, "We just don't give up, we don't quit." He was right, but every now and then, for my mental state, it would be good to have a game that wasn't always a comeback win – but I was not complaining.

34

LEARNING TO FLY

The morning of Cody's presentation to Centennial's English classes, I asked him how he was doing. I wanted reassurance that he was emotionally okay. He was clear that he knew his boundaries with the students and himself. He was actively practicing his coping skills. It was not that I didn't realize it before, but it became very evident as Cody headed out that morning that speaking was becoming his passion. He needed to speak. He was drawn to speak. He was telling a story that most would not feel comfortable sharing. I could barely talk about it, let alone share my pain in front of people. Here he was, out there, shining light into the darkness. He was spreading hope.

I have often asked myself, *Why Cody? Why our family?* That's pretty selfish, isn't it? It feels like a particularly selfish way of thinking as I type it out and see it in black and white. Knowing it was selfish caused me to ask a stronger question: *Why not us?* We were not immune to a mental health illness or crisis. I was beginning to see a new, clearer picture laid out in front of me regarding my son. It was as if Cody was able to speak for those who couldn't speak, the ones who were lost or too afraid of what people would think if they spoke their truth. He was becoming their advocate. By sharing his story, he was drawing more attention to those who needed help.

I was familiar with Cody's outline of his presentation. He would provide the backstory of his life, then educational information about depression and anxiety. He would discuss symptoms, and the difference between looking happy and feeling happy. He used a visual graph to explain the difference between happy and sad and normal and depressed. I liked how he described different types of depression. There is short-lived depression, for example how you might feel when you get a bad test grade; and then there is being depressed for longer than two weeks, which can be a place of despair and hopelessness. He would talk about his inpatient experience, tools he learned and the treatment options. He addressed the importance of sleep, exercise, relaxation and a healthy diet. He talked about dealing with expectations, and would conclude with techniques for handling dark thoughts. He used an "annoying relative" analogy: the annoying relative may come to visit, but they will leave. He'd then allow time for a Q&A and give details about where to go if you needed help.

Cody is modest and doesn't talk about himself. He has always been that way. So I had to drag how the presentation went out of him. He was content with how his presentation had gone, but had been excited by the interaction during the Q&A. Students openly talked about their emotional struggles and asked for more information on coping skills and treatment options. Students had been given a sheet of paper on which they could write their questions down and also give constructive feedback for future presentations. These were then handed to the teacher to allow privacy for the students and to also allow the teacher to screen the questions for Cody as there were certain areas that were off limits. The method of his attempted suicide is one of them; Cody would not talk about that. Cody was impressed with their questions, which were clear and direct. They wanted more information about mental health conditions and more information on treatment options and where to go for help. Overall, they had felt Cody's sincerity and had appreciated his honesty and truthfulness.

The three points from Cody's presentation that resounded most with the students were: *Keeping something locked in will not help anything, but will only make the problem grow. Treat dark thoughts like a relative who comes to visit, they will go away. Success should be measured by happiness and not money; do what makes you happy.*

They had also found it helpful to learn about different coping skills, and they would have liked to hear more on Cody's individual healing process. Cody felt he could make some of those changes for next time.

The following day, Nicole called to share how impactful Cody's presentation was. It had resonated with her students on a peer level. Cody spoke right into their world. He was authentic, real and caring. She had witnessed something powerful. She told me that they hadn't had the opportunity to have a student-to-student discussion at this level before, and now they were talking and sharing their secrets more openly; they were feeling safer. I could barely take in all the feedback she was giving me. She had been so excited to see the difference it made to her students.

Other teachers wanted to have Cody come and speak to their classes, but he couldn't fit it in his schedule between schoolwork, baseball and senior year activities. We had no idea that Cody and Nicole would go on to work together again on a much bigger scale. For now the focus was school, baseball and graduation.

35

A CINDERELLA TEAM –
YOU CAN'T MAKE THIS STUFF UP

Our play-in game against Wilson ended in a 3-0 win for the Pioneers. Our pitcher threw a one-hitter with nine strikeouts. We were now in the Class 5A State baseball playoffs.

The important part of this season for me on a personal level was how Cody was doing emotionally. I'd been fooled before and didn't want to take any chances. As much as we were all having fun with the season, Cody's health was my number one priority. I would check in with him on a regular basis, but his continued response was, "I'm good, excited for the team, but keeping everything in perspective."

The next game was away against Madison. Madison was Portland's Interscholastic League Champion. They had taken the State Title in 2012. Their starting pitcher hadn't given up an earned run since the end of March. The Pioneers did get some love from one news article that said not to count Sandy out, but we were not expected to win.

You wouldn't know that by the way we played, however. Our ace pitcher was lights out; Cody shared that it was the best game he'd ever seen Carson throw in his life. The Pioneers had 13 hits that led us to a 12-0 win, including a three-run homer by Bryce, our shortstop.

Marist was our next opponent, and they had already defeated one of the top seeds. We would get to play on our home field.

And we had thought that Senior Night would be our last home game! I'm glad we were wrong. I knew this next game would be packed out because it was on our home turf, so we arrived 90 minutes early to get seats. Excitement filled the air. You could smell the hot dogs and hamburgers on the barbecue, along with the wonderful smell of popcorn. The teams were doing their warm-up and I could see Cody doing his crazy talent of juggling a bat and two baseballs. I happened to catch him in the act and got it on video. I cherish those moments, like when Dana performed her last floor routine before she retired from competitive gymnastics. They are memories that stay imprinted forever.

I was given permission by the coach to continue with the candy bars. He wasn't about to mess with breaking a tradition. The only change I made was to have full-size candy bars. During the season, Cody and some of the other players had started growing mustaches. Fans brought banners and signs to the game reflecting their show of support. Dana had Cody's number painted on her back. The fans were in full force. If we won, our next game would be against Sherwood, our nemesis, on their home field.

This game came with an extra-large dose of stress. The Pioneers started the seventh inning with a 2-1 lead. All we needed was three outs and we were moving on. The umpire was struggling behind the plate, and Sandy was not getting fair calls to close out the inning. Darin, our number two pitcher, threw a strike that would have closed the inning, but the umpire called a ball. Cody lost his temper and said loudly, "That was a strike and you know it." Never have I witnessed Cody ever lose his temper in all his years playing baseball or any other sport. Darin hadn't been getting any calls, and Cody knew this game should be over. Cody's behavior told me that the umpire was calling a horrific game.

For a brief moment I thought he may get thrown out of the game and I almost couldn't contain myself in my seat. It was extremely tense. Coach quickly walked out onto the field to talk to the umpire and give Cody time to cool off. I could feel my heart racing.

At that moment, Coach made a decision he would come to apologize for later: he pulled Darin and put Carson in. You could see it in the team's faces. They didn't agree, but knew the decision was made. Darin wanted to finish the game, and Carson who had just pitched was not pleased. Darin was moved to third to replace Carson. The infield gathered round Carson and had a meeting on the mound. It was undetermined if they could get back in the right headspace to win this game. I felt like throwing up.

Marist was able to tie up the game before their final out. It was now into extra innings. Our second baseman, Mitchell, opened up the eighth inning with a two-strike single and then our shortstop, Bryce, followed with a sacrifice bunt that advanced Mitchell to second, a scoring position. Marist then pulled their pitcher. Their new pitcher hit our next two batters. The bases were loaded.

So, here we were again. Cody was up to bat. Yes, I saw it coming, and yes, I felt both excited and ready to crawl out of my skin. I couldn't make eye contact with anyone. I could hear the crowd yelling, "Welty, come on deuces, let's go 22." All my emotions were colliding. Coach pulled Cody aside, whispered something and Cody responded back, but I couldn't tell what was said. I was concerned with the amount of pressure he would be feeling. I couldn't keep my eyes off him. He looked calm and ready. *Why couldn't I be that calm?* He took the first two pitches for balls, then a called strike and another ball. I held my breath. The final pitch left the pitcher's hands and it felt as if it moved in slow motion. It was low and outside, the umpire called a ball. Cody ran down to first base expressively clapping and celebrating as Mitchell ran and touched home plate. It was another walk-off win.

There was mayhem in the crowd; you could have heard those cheers from miles away. After crossing home plate, Mitchell came running to grab Cody as the rest of the team surged out of the dugout in pursuit of another pile on. I mentally took a snapshot of that moment. His last at bat on the field where, a year before, he had been in so much pain and where, after a baseball game just like this, we had almost lost him. It didn't even seem real. My soul ached but was rejoicing. It took time for the crowd to calm and for the congratulations to be over before I could share the treats with the team. Our family stayed and watched for the final time as Cody and his teammates finished the field maintenance.

After the game, I asked Cody what Coach had said to him. He smiled and said, "He just wanted to make sure I was okay, and I said yes. I then told him, 'I'm going to take one strike, I've got this coach.'" Coach shared that Cody went up there with an absolutely perfect approach, and that Coach knew he was going to come through for the team. He could see it in Cody's eyes. Mitchell added, "We live to fight another day. This isn't the last game we get to play."

This was the first time in program history that the baseball program was going to the state semi-finals.

36

FACING THE GIANTS

Game day arrived. Will took the afternoon off work and we pulled Dana early from school. The game was set for 4:30pm and it took an hour to get to Sherwood, and we didn't want to risk any traffic issues. We were all a little edgy and anxious. Will even checked I had the candy bars for the boys. Which, of course, I did – I had packed those first. This was going to be a battle. Sherwood's team was stacked, including a player who went on to have a successful college career and become the number one first overall draft pick in the MLB (Major League Baseball).

We weren't the first to arrive, even though we were there an hour before the game. We set our blanket down and decided to walk off some nervous energy. I would always try to make eye contact with Cody before the game. It was important for me to let him know we were there. Not that he didn't think we would be, but it was a superstition of mine. As game time approached, I took in the scene all around me. The amount of fan support was overwhelming. Friends, family, students, teachers, coaching staff and administrators had all made the time to drive the distance and support our team. Many had brought decorated fan posters. I felt part of something special.

The newspaper had predicted an epic pitching duel. They were right. As the game got underway, both teams got runners on base but each pitcher and good defense stopped any runs from scoring. That was until the top of the fifth. Our DH (designated hitter), Rhett, started off the inning with a single. Then a couple of batters later, Mitchell, our second baseman, was up to bat. He had done well at the plate against their pitcher earlier on in the season. Coach went with a hunch and called a hit and run. It couldn't have been done more beautifully. Rhett was already heading to second as the ball left the pitcher's hands. Mitchell had a bat of his life, by smacking a fast ball over the first baseman's head. Because Rhett was already running at the time of the hit, he was able to make it home standing up on Mitchell's double.

The screaming from our fans sounded like we had three times the amount of people there. The dugout exploded in roars. It was thrilling. This game was far from over, but we drew first blood on an aggressive play. Sherwood sat stunned. I do not believe they ever saw that play coming. The tables had turned and the Pioneers were in the driver's seat, you could feel it in the air. Carson had the wind at his back and retired their next three batters.

Sherwood ended up pulling their ace pitcher, but we continued to score. After another two singles, Mitch did it again, with a shot over the head of Sherwood's right fielder. It was 3-0 at the top of the sixth. Sherwood scored in the bottom of the sixth, but then we scored again in the top of the seventh to make it 6-1. Sherwood pulled within three runs but had two outs. We needed one more out. Carson had two strikes on the batter. We were all standing at this point. His next pitch was a curveball in the dirt. The batter had swung, but because it went into the dirt before it reached Cody's mitt, the batter was allowed to run and try to make it to first base before the catcher threw him out. Cody scooped the ball but knew the runner was too far away to tag him, so he took the inside line and – as per his words – shot put it to the first baseman so as to not overthrow the throw. Austin caught the ball before the runner made it to first. We had won! The Pioneers side of the field erupted in elation. The Sherwood fans were stunned.

The sound of our crowd's celebration surrounded every corner of the space around me. The screams of victory overtook us. Cody threw his catcher's mitt in the air and ran out to embrace Carson. The team was screaming and hugging each other. Electricity filled the air. I looked around and I could see tears flowing, heads shaking in disbelief, high fives flying and bodies jumping.

Everyone stayed until the boys came out of the dugout. They were mobbed by friends and family. Cody and the other players kept saying, "I can't believe this is happening, we're going to the State Championship." It was hard to leave the field. Everyone wanted to stay there talking, but there was a bus waiting to take the players home. I ran to my car and grabbed the candy and gave it to Cody through the bus window. The boys had their heads out talking to all of us as they were about to leave. It was quite the sight – smiles from ear to ear. To be a mouse on that bus and listen to the chatter would have been priceless. We listened to Macklemore, "My, Oh My" on repeat on the way home. It is one of our family songs.

The State Championship was to take place in four days' time and our opponents would be Hood River.

37

THE FINAL GAME

I woke up early that day because Jenni and I were preparing lunches for the boys to take on the bus to Salem. It was strange to think this was the last game our boys would play in together. The game would start at 2pm at Keizer Stadium in Salem and we would be the home team.

I got home in plenty of time to make Cody some breakfast and send him off with as much good luck as I could. A tailgate picnic was organized for a few hours before the game, so we were leaving early. It took about an hour to get to the field and we still needed to get some food and drink for the picnic. I had already grabbed the candy bars – I had chosen King Size Milk Duds and brought a Sharpie along to write on each box either "Amazing Season" or "State Champions". The weather looked perfect – high seventies and sunny. I decided to buy fake mustaches for friends, family and anyone else who wanted one to wear to give Cody a shout out for the mustache he had grown. His own superstition was that he would not shave it off until after the season – he had had no idea the season would go on so long.

After the picnic, we headed to the stadium and got our seats. The field looked large compared to our high school field and you could feel the day getting warmer. We decided to put on the mustaches as the Pioneers took infield practice – we were quite a sight. Cody walked out and looked for us in the stands, and when he realized what he was seeing he gave us a big smile and nodded his head in approval.

The Pioneers' fan section was packed. Music was playing over the loudspeaker and it felt like we were at a big league game. Warm-ups were done and the Pioneers took the field as we were the home team and would have final ups.

Hood River came ready to play. Three of the first five batters had singles and our defense, which had been strong all season, made a couple of errors that allowed Hood River to score three by the time the inning ended. We seemed to be too amped up. It was our turn at bat. The Pioneers were able to gain two runs back in the bottom of that inning but were still behind by one. It was an important comeback for the team – they didn't let that bad inning define their attitudes and direction of the game. They were fighting back.

Carson settled in and the next inning Hood River could not get a hit. Before the top of the third inning started, Dana came up to me and within seconds I knew what was happening: she was having an allergy attack. Her eyes were swollen and she couldn't stop sneezing. She looked awful. I grabbed the Benadryl in my purse that I always have for these situations and we headed to the bathroom – I have found that it helps sometimes to try and wash the allergens off. We washed her face, hands and arms, and wet down her hair. I thought to myself, *Oh my gosh if this doesn't get better, I'm going to need to take her to urgent care.* She had had an episode like this when she was little at a baseball tournament and Benadryl had worked that time. My heart started to race again. I was trying to quickly determine what I should do. My anxiety was rising. I silently prayed for her and just asked for calmness. I was ready to leave this game if needed. There was no way I was taking a risk with her. Dana could read my signals.

She just looked at me and said she was going to be okay. I gave her a questioning look and said, "I'll give it 15 minutes to work and if you're not better we're heading to urgent care."

I was taken right back to that night when I hadn't heard from Cody and had told Will I'd give him 15 minutes before I lost my shit. I started to get emotional, and just wanted to cry. Dana didn't want to leave the game, and nor did I, but we both knew we may have to – life happens. I have come to realize that life doesn't always work out the way we might like, even if we do everything right. Life is just messy. There would be nothing I could do but monitor her for the next 15 minutes.

As we walked back to our seats, my niece Courtney was also having an allergy attack. My other niece Tori pulled out her children's liquid Benadryl, as I had already used up our emergency supply. What was happening? Then somebody pointed out that a huge field across the highway had just been mown and it was blowing our way. I started to worry that Cody would also have a reaction, and then I remembered he had his medical kit in his baseball bag. Cody was allergic to nuts, so he had an EPI pen and Benadryl wherever he went. Later, we found out that Cody did get a couple of hives on his arm and Kyle, our left fielder, was also struggling with his allergies during the game.

As the third inning continued, I could see that Dana's allergies were subsiding, as were Courtney's. Thank God.

It was now the bottom of the fifth and getting stressful. I knew we only had three more at bats to gain numbers on the scoreboard. This inning was the game changer. We had runners on first and second and two outs. Carson, under pressure of two strikes, hit a shot that flew over the shortstop and our runner on second scored. We had tied the game. The crowd went wild. The two out rally continued with two more runs scored, putting us on top. An error by Hood River allowed one more run to score. We were up 6-3 at the end of the inning. The Pioneers were able to keep Hood River from scoring their next at bats.

It was the bottom of the sixth and, as Cody was making his way to the batter's box, Will and I looked at each other. We both knew that this could be Cody's last at bat. He had already made the decision to not attempt to play college ball. I tuned everything out and focused on all the little details of his at bat. I was beyond grateful and in awe of how far he had come – for him to be at this place in baseball was more than I could ever have imagined or hoped. He ended his baseball career with a nice shot to left field that was caught.

Before the inning ended, the Pioneers had gained two more runs. The score was now 8-3 heading into the final inning. We needed three outs.

During the space between innings, music is always played. "Sweet Caroline" by Neil Diamond came on and all of us on the Sandy sidelines stood up and began singing. "Sweet Caroline" is by far one of the most iconic baseball songs out there; it gives me goosebumps every time. The boys came out and raised their arms up to us as they took to the field. They could feel it too. They were so close.

Hood River was able to get two base runners on but had two outs. We were all standing at this moment. Carson threw a pitch that the batter popped up to the right side just over the head of Austin, our first baseman. Austin headed in the direction of the ball, which flew toward the Hood River dugout. I couldn't tell if it was catchable. The crowd was silent as we watched Austin extend his body over the railing of their dugout and reach out his arm to make the game-winning catch. We won! The silence was suddenly filled with an eruption of the fans' emotional screams.

I tried to focus on so many things at once, I didn't want to miss any of it. Cameras flashing, boys racing around with mitts flying in the air, the pile up, family and friends hugging, and all the while tears streamed down my face as my hand covered my mouth in awe of what I had just witnessed. My girlfriend Jenni took one look at me and pulled me in for a hug. She knew this season almost didn't happen for us. I could have cried and cried. I could hardly catch my breath. It was overwhelming. Hope, healing, teamwork, redemption and renewed relationships resonated this whole season. The underdogs, the Cinderella team, the inexperienced. This was a comeback season as good as any I have ever seen, a comeback for so many. I have always said that you can never put a limit on the power of the human spirit. Amazing things can happen. Cody ended his career with two hits and an RBI and a State Championship. Carson pitched an amazing game and the team never gave up; as Coach said later, "Everyone did something to help us get here."

The boys were like little kids. They could barely contain their excitement as they stood in the line waiting to have their individual medals draped round their neck. Then the 5A State Championship trophy was presented to the team. The boys ran and all together held the trophy high in the air with their fingers showing the #1 sign. Cameras were flashing everywhere. This is what movies are made of I thought to myself. After the presentation, they headed into their last team huddle with their coaches. This was my chance. I ran to my car to get the Milk Duds. I quickly wrote "State Champions" on each box as my hand shook. I then ran the candy bars to their bus driver and asked if he would hand one to each boy as they got on the bus. He was excited to do so. The fun in baseball was alive. I couldn't wait to get back to the action in the stadium.

The fans had created a long line to congratulate each player as they made their way out of the dugout and up the stadium bleachers. On my way to the celebration line, a parent from last season, who didn't have a boy playing this year, stopped me. He didn't say a word, and I could tell he was about ready to cry, he just gave me the most tender hug. That spoke so much to me. I knew he understood what Cody had been through and what this season meant to him.

After all the celebrations, the boys headed out to the bus and an impromptu dinner was planned with the team and any parents who could make it. It was a nice ending to the day. There would be a big celebration team dinner after graduation week. I asked the coach if I could put together a slideshow of the season and offered to host the dinner at our house. I had no idea at the time how much work that would be – thankfully my niece Alyssa knew what she was doing.

It was hard to sleep that night after we had spent the whole evening recapping the season and realizing that their team were State Champions.

It was fun to read the newspaper and hear some of the highlights. We were considered the Cinderella team as we had had one of the biggest turnarounds the state had seen in a while. The paper talked about how Sandy had not been on the map of the teams predicted to win. It was, however, the first time in history that Sandy High School's baseball team won a Championship and, at nine, we were the lowest seed to win a baseball state championship. It was an amazing ride, but by no means an end to our story.

The team put Cody's jersey in the dugout for the rest of the baseball season after they heard what happened.

Dana and I at my Run Girlfriend Run event, two weeks after Cody's attempt. I actually don't remember much about that day.

Cody's first time back on the baseball field, catching for Carson. Late summer 2013.

Sandy High School 5A State Championship Team, June 2014.

From the Youth Suicide Prevention Forum, October 7th, 2015. Top: Galli making the introduction presentation in the auditorium. Above: Cody during his part of the presentation sharing his story.

Trip to Tucson, AZ to get Cody settled in to start his PhD program, 2018.

From the Out of the Darkness Walk for suicide prevention at Western Oregon University in May 2019 when Cody spoke.

38

MY TURN

Cody graduated high school and Dana survived freshman year. Cody was to start a major in criminal justice and minor in psychology at Western Oregon University in the fall.

Summer had its struggles as Cody stretched his boundaries for freedom and my fear elevated. I discovered a marijuana stash and realized he was drinking at times. I think if we didn't have the suicide attempt in our past, I may have been more balanced with my reactions. I was afraid that he was using alcohol or marijuana as a coping mechanism.

I struggled with not having the structure of school and sports to keep tabs on Cody's comings and goings. I've never been a so-called helicopter mom, but I was definitely exhibiting signs of one now. The new territory I was attempting to maneuver through wasn't going as well as it should. I was building walls of safety around my family, and my attempt to control situations out of fear was unhealthy. Cody was 18 years old, about to head off to college and he needed to spread his wings. I needed to figure out how to let go while managing my fear of missing a relapse. There were painful but necessary conversations between us. It was a difficult time of self-discovery as a parent. These conversations allowed me to see how growing up with an alcoholic father was now dictating so much of my underlying fear, and it was affecting my parenting. I needed to ask myself how I may have contributed to any of the pressures that Cody felt.

Viper: "The simple fact is you feel responsible for Goose and you have a confidence problem. Now I'm not gonna sit here and blow sunshine up your ass, Lieutenant. A good pilot is compelled to evaluate what's happened, so he can apply what he's learned. Up there, we gotta push it. That's our job. It's your option, Lieutenant. All yours."

There is a scene in the film *Top Gun* where Maverick is talking to his commanding officer, Viper, about losing his friend in a plane crash that explains what I was feeling.

I felt responsible and I had a confidence problem. My guilt was blinding every decision and action and dictating my behavior. I needed to evaluate what had happened, learn from it and make any necessary changes. I had to face my guilt and see what was behind it so I could move through it.

I noticed how difficult it was for me to watch the news or hear stories of mental health crises. I didn't understand why the rest of my family could hear or see the stories and were able to put them in perspective. I, however, had to leave the room. I needed help walking through the process. I needed counseling.

I found a female counselor who had experience with suicide and was taking new clients. Our first meeting was tougher emotionally than I was prepared for. She asked me to put into words how I was doing. I couldn't. It's as if I was hiding something that I didn't know I was hiding. All I could convey was that I felt I'd lost my way in this new life. I knew I didn't belong in my old life prior to May 1st, 2013, but I didn't belong in this new life either. I was in limbo, trying to find my new normal. The past haunted me and my future was surrounded in anxiety and caution. I was usually a very expressive and touchy-feely person, but I wasn't comfortable acting that way anymore and I didn't know why. Wonderful things were happening in our lives, but I was stuck. I felt like the ball in the pinball machine, bouncing from one emotion to the next and never finding a safe spot to land.

As I tried to share, I started to cry. I had difficulty formulating a clear thought process. I would stop in mid-sentence as I physically couldn't get the next words out. There was a block. She let me fumble through the stops and starts. I kept apologizing, saying, "It's already been over a year, I don't know what is wrong with me." She was calm and said very slowly and gently, "Have you ever allowed yourself to tell your story of this experience or talk about your pain?"

I thought before I responded. *I have talked with the other mom and friends and family. It's not like I don't cry, but I fear going too deep, so I stop myself. I feel guilty for giving myself the attention. I bury anything that resembles pain and tell myself I'll get to it later. I hold on to everyone else's coattails as they head down the road of healing. I can only get so far with the healing process before I step back.*

I looked up at her, exhausted from my own head talk. She patiently waited for me to talk. I conveyed that I didn't think I had spoken about it in the way she was asking – it felt too painful and I was afraid of what might come out. She understood, and asked if I would be willing to try. I nodded yes and she asked me to start from the beginning.

It took a minute for me to allow myself to let go, but then I must have talked non-stop for the remainder of the session. Thank God she had planned extra time for our visit. I don't know if I could have physically stopped talking once I had started. It was a tidal wave of words pouring out of me. She helped me understand the importance of continuing to talk about my experiences, even if I was repeating myself and the stories. In time, the need to tell the story and talk about the experience would dissipate. She gave me encouragement that, as I continued to heal and work through my own struggles, I would come to a point where they wouldn't dictate every thought I had or dictate every decision I made.

Over the course of my time with her, I learned new coping skills to address my PTSD and fear. She helped me work through the massive hill of guilt I felt that I failed my children.

She helped me slowly build back my confidence as a parent. I stayed in counseling for six months and, by the end, I was more comfortable in my new emotional skin. Counseling worked for me, it felt natural and not rushed. I needed someone outside my circle of friends and family to confide in and help me professionally through my struggles. I didn't have to be strong with her or prove myself, I could just be me.

Counseling was difficult and painful, but it is fulfilling when you see yourself work through an obstacle and experience freedom. It is a wonderful feeling to smash fears, face your demons and win a battle. I had setbacks, but I learned how to get up from them and try again. I wasn't stuck anymore. I was more assured of myself that, as other issues may arise with Cody, Dana or Will, I would be better prepared to face the battle. I didn't do this part of recovering alone. I had to enlist the help of my family to practice my tools and ask for grace as I tested out new boundaries for them and myself. I didn't always succeed the first time out with my new skills, but I could see improvement and so could they.

39

A COLLEGE "MAJOR" SHIFT

Cody and his doctor agreed to maintain his current dosage of antidepressants during his transition to college. If all was going well, then weaning off could take place during Christmas break. Fortunately, the transition to college went smoothly. Cody was rooming with a buddy from school, which gave me some peace of mind. We agreed to Skype every Sunday to say hello. We called it SOS (Skype on Sunday). It was important for me that Cody and Dana stayed close, and this allowed us a dedicated space to do that. I wanted Cody involved in Dana's life and Dana involved in his, and this was a great use of technology to do that.

Life began to move along in more of a normal pattern. Dana was enjoying school and cross-country, and Cody was adapting to college life. I thought that we had finally crossed the bridge to the other side of our journey, and that the climax to this story had been reached. I was wrong. Something bigger was coming, and it was bigger than Cody's individual story of recovery.

In March 2015, during Cody's spring term and almost three years after his suicide attempt, Cody called to tell me that he had to read a book in his psychology class called *Surrounded by Darkness*. He shared that he wasn't looking forward to it. It was about a mother's journey with her daughter with mental illness. I understood his concern, but also encouraged him that it could bring some more healing. He hesitantly agreed. His goal was to read it soon and he promised he'd reach out with an update. I put it aside in my mind, knowing he would call when he was ready.

What I didn't know was that the phone call would come at 3am later in the same week.

I was sound asleep when I heard our phone ringing. I panicked and sat straight up in bed.

Will answered and I could hear Cody's voice on the other end, "Dad, I'm okay I just need to talk with Mom." Will handed me the phone.

I was now wide awake.

"Cody, what's wrong?" I said cautiously.

Cody calmly replied, "Mom, I'm really okay, I just got done reading the book, I couldn't put it down."

There was a pause and then he said, so tenderly, "I'm just calling to tell you I'm sorry for what I put you through."

I started to tear up, and said, "Cody, it's okay, it's okay."

"Mom, I just want to make sure you're okay," he said.

I was honest when I replied, "Cody, I am okay. I'm not telling you it wasn't rough, but I have my faith, our family and friends that have been my support through this. That is so sweet that you called."

He shared how much the book meant to him. He wanted me to read it, I suggested he email the author and let her know what the book meant to him. He thought that was a good idea and said he'd do that. We said we loved each other and hung up the phone.

Will looked at me and asked, "You okay?"

I confidently replied, "Yes, you know why? Because he called me at three in the morning. He knew I wouldn't care what time he called, and he knew he needed to talk and reached out." It was the perfect example of him using what he had learned.

It took a while for me to drift back off to sleep, but I did. My alarm went off at 6:15am. I grabbed my phone, there was a text message from Cody. He asked me to check my email. He had decided to email the author that morning and she had replied to him within an hour. He shared the email exchange with me.

Hi Rachel, my name is Cody Welty. I am a student at Western Oregon University and am currently taking a psychology course that requires the reading of your book. At first, I was hesitant. I personally suffer from mental illness and wondered what I could possibly get out of a book depicting the life of someone like me. Then I started reading. I didn't know I could connect emotionally to a story of someone's life until now. Your story about your mother and daughter reminded me so much of my life, and what I've put my own mother through. I never thought it was okay to talk about being depressed as a young male athlete, and also felt like the system of how mental illness is treated is flawed. As hard as it was for me to read through your book without breaking down into relapses of the depressed lifestyle that I suffered only a few years ago, I want to thank you for sharing your story and acknowledging that talking about mental illness is a good thing. I currently speak to some high schools around Oregon about my personal story as well as anxiety and depression. I wanted to send this email to thank you for sharing your story with the world. My mother and I have also agreed that the best way to heal is to talk. Again, thank you Rachel, and I hope in the future I can meet with you sometime to express my thanks that someone else is working toward a better system for mental illness. You are a hero to many families like mine. I hope you receive this email, and I wish you the best.

***

Your note brought tears to my eyes. To have touched a young person like you is humbling and inspiring. I'm sorry for the pain you've gone through with your own mental illness, but delighted to know that you're not keeping secrets. We need to learn so much about mental illness. It is by telling our stories that change will happen. I too hope we will meet some day.

I immediately called Cody after reading the emails. I was excited for him. It was this book and other situations like this that confirmed for Cody the need to change his major from Criminal Justice to Psychology and to minor in Biology. His desire to make a difference in the mental health community became his mission and passion. He wanted to understand the science behind the psychology and devote his life to helping youths like himself. He wanted to find ways to make a difference in the field of mental health.

Later, I did read the book Cody asked me to and was glad I did. Even though it was painful, it was a powerful read. It helped me understand the impact it had on Cody and why he was moved to call me that night at 3am.

40

SPEAKING THE UNSPEAKABLE

No matter how strong you think you are, you'll never be
stronger than the moment you ask for help.
Cody Welty

During the summer of 2015, Nicole, the teacher from Centennial High School, reached out to Cody again. She was now a principal at Cedar Ridge Middle School in Sandy, and she wanted to know if Cody was willing to share his story with her middle school students in conjunction with some mental health awareness. He was excited for the opportunity to further the message. They worked on a presentation outline, and the plan was for him to speak toward the middle of September before he went back to college.

Concurrently, I received an email from Julia, the Communications Director for our school district who had received a request from Galli Murray of Clackamas County Behavioral Health regarding a call to action in youth suicide prevention. They were looking for a couple of courageous young people willing to share their story of attempted suicide in a forum setting. Julia thought Cody may be interested in being a presenter. I immediately forwarded the email to Cody. After reading the email, Cody not only was willing to share his story, but became extremely interested in the work the county was doing. Julia connected Galli with Cody and the two of them set up a face-to-face meeting.

During their meeting, Galli explained how she had been recently hired as the county's first youth suicide prevention coordinator. The goal of the forum was to kick-start a new suicide prevention initiative in Clackamas County. Having a speaker who had survived a suicide attempt would allow the audience to glean helpful information to help the county's youth. Cody would be joining a panel of specialists from around the region who would speak about the data, programs and different ways to support youth. They were also gathering 52 volunteers who would wear a sweatshirt that said, "Ask the Question". Those volunteers would represent the 52 lives lost each year to suicide in Clackamas County.

Cody and Galli hit it off and he agreed to be a presenter. He also asked if I would be willing to be one of the 52 volunteers. I agreed. The date was set for October 7th. Cody was glad to have his presentation at Cedar Ridge prior to the forum, to give him some more experience of speaking in front of a crowd and fine-tune his talk. Over time, Galli and Cody would come to be a familiar pair in the mental health community for youth suicide prevention awareness.

On the morning of September 17th, 2015, Cody had his presentation in the gymnasium of Cedar Ridge Middle School, titled "Speaking the Unspeakable – Mental Illness and Recovery". Cody went ahead of us to do final preparations with Nicole. This was the first time Will and I saw him speak. We were both nervous for him. This was a much bigger audience than the classrooms he had presented in before. We arrived about 15 minutes early to get checked in and find out where we would be seated. I think each school smells the same way, and once we walked in, I had a flood of memories rush in of being back in middle school. The noise of student activity hovered in the background as the two office staff checked us in and thanked us for coming. They made a point of expressing how brave Cody was. We smiled and nodded as we grabbed our visitor lanyards and put them round our necks. They pointed toward the gym and said we could take seats in the back bleachers. We walked in and saw Cody talking with Nicole, and we waved at each other. He was standing next to a podium that was situated in the middle of a large semicircle of chairs. He would be making two presentations. One specifically for sixth graders and another for the seventh and eighth graders.

Proud isn't a big enough word to describe my feelings for what Cody was about to do. It was bravery at its finest. What most people don't know is that public speaking is hard for Cody. He's become more relaxed over time, but in the beginning it was rough on him. Nevertheless, he was determined to get the message across. He has always made it clear that he chose to speak because he didn't want others to end up where he did. He wanted mental illness to become something people could talk about.

Nicole prepared her students well. She opened up the presentation by sharing with the children that everyone around you may be fighting a battle that you may know nothing about – so it's important to be kind. She also emphasized that anyone can be affected by stress, anxiety and depression. She then did a wonderful job introducing Cody. The students became silent as Cody walked up to the podium. I could feel myself holding my breath. Will must have noticed my tension, because he reached over gently and held my hand. I quietly let my breath out and listened to my son.

Cody shared how he had experienced depression and the steps he took to overcome it. He shared how people will ask him if he sees suicide as a problem or a solution. He looks at suicide as a poor solution to the problem of depression. You can't stop suicide without first dealing with depression. He addressed stigmas, positive and negative coping skills, and places to go for help. He then left time at the end for a Q&A.

The questions being asked by these students made me pause. So many of these young ones were in pain, and they wanted to share their stories. Nicole had to come in to wrap up the Q&As during both sessions as the students could have kept going. Teachers were dotted throughout the gym ready to help any children who might need to talk afterward. Many students stayed to talk directly with Cody and to thank him for coming. They didn't feel alone now, they saw someone like them. I realize you may think depression doesn't start this early in middle school, but it does – I witnessed it.

An article about the presentation ended up in our local newspaper that week. It was the first time Cody's own personal story was in print. It was strange and wonderful to see my son's picture in the paper not related to sports. Cody received numerous comments of thanks for his bravery and for his willingness to tell his story. It had made an impact. I was grateful when I would hear from parents whose students were at the presentation that Cody's story opened a dialogue between parent and child that hadn't happened before.

A couple of weeks after the presentation, I received an envelope from Jenni that was given to her from Brock. At some point, Jenni had given a copy of the newspaper article about Cody to Brock, who ended up writing Cody a letter and including a copy of his journal notes from the night he saved him. I told Jenni to let Brock know I'd give the envelope to Cody. The crazy part was the next time I was going to see him was at the upcoming forum.

I remembered back when Brock told me that when he was ready he would share his journal notes with Cody. I held an envelope in my hand that would give me even more insight into what happened that night, and I hoped Cody would let me read it someday.

41

ASK THE QUESTION

We are not hopeless, we are not powerless and we are not weak. We can all ask for help when we need it. We can all do our best to help end suicide.

Cody Welty

The day of the forum arrived. Dana wasn't able to come because of school, but Will took the day off from work. I was grateful for this, as I wanted as much support for Cody as possible. Cody wasn't riding with us as he would be coming directly from college.

Will and I arrived at the community center where the forum was to take place. They had asked the volunteers to arrive early to get us set up for our part of the event. After entering the lobby, we followed the signage directing us upstairs. I immediately saw the check-in area for the volunteers. Will waited in the large foyer as I made my way over to the table where two women sat. I gave them my name, received my blue hooded sweatshirt and was given an overview of what to expect. After I was done, I joined Will in an area out of the way of all the activity.

I kept looking toward the staircase for Cody. More and more people were arriving. I started to worry he was stuck in traffic when I saw him round the landing on the staircase. He looked relaxed and calm. I, however, was not. I was anxious for too many reasons to count. He gave me a big hug, and that alone helped me feel more at ease. I needed to know and feel he was doing okay. It was within those few seconds that a woman with a huge smile started to approach us. Cody reached out and gave her a hug. He then introduced us to Galli. I immediately fell in love with her. She couldn't say enough about how brave Cody was and how much she enjoyed working with him on this project. You could tell they were forming a special bond.

She told us passionately about the work that Clackamas County was doing with suicide prevention. Her desire with this forum was to reduce the stigma of mental health and promote education with the hope of decreasing suicides in Clackamas County through mental health first-aid training and suicide prevention trainings.

There would be three mental health professionals on the panel with Cody; they included state and county specialists from the behavioral and public health fields. The audience would host a variety of individuals, including service and healthcare providers, school staff, individuals with related life experience and members of the faith community, along with some spaces open to the general public. The forum was predicted to last two hours.

Cody would be the third speaker out of the four. They would be filming the presentation and the news media would be there to cover the program. She provided me more detail regarding the sweatshirt I had been given to wear. It had the words, "Ask the Question" in big letters on the back, and the 52 volunteers wearing these sweatshirts were going to be invited onto the stage at the end of the presentation to represent those lives lost to suicide each year in Clackamas County.

It was getting close to kick-off time and Cody and Galli needed to get ready. I wished them good luck and Will and I headed to our assigned seats. Will sat below me as I was up with the group wearing the sweatshirts.

The auditorium was filling up fast. I hadn't realized so many people would be here. Before long, the room was filled to capacity (approximately 170 people) – they even had to turn people away! Cody sat among these experts and I couldn't have been more in awe of him. What I was seeing showed that something wonderful can come out of something that was initially devastating. I couldn't have foreseen his path – no way!

I was sitting in between two women. One woman casually asked me why I had volunteered. I turned to look at her as I pointed to Cody on the panel, "I'm his mom. He is speaking on behalf of youth." I thought to myself, *Oh geez, I hope this isn't going to get weird.* I wasn't sure if that had been the best way to respond. The woman on the other side of me heard the conversation and said, "He's a brave young man," and the original woman nodded. I smiled in agreement. My gift of speaking quickly on my feet went out the door when speaking about mental health. I was still learning and didn't feel confident with my explanations.

The two speakers before Cody focused on the statistics of youth suicide in Oregon, as well as on the Zero Suicide initiative[5] which Clackamas county had not at that point embraced but would, just weeks following the forum. We learned that suicide was the second leading cause of death for 10- to 24-year-olds, second to car fatalities.

It was Cody's turn. One thing I appreciate in Cody's presentations is his ability to use humor in a positive way with a dark topic. He's able to add that because he's been there, it works for him. He started by telling his own survival story and then walked through his recovery process. He emphasized the need for a mechanism that allows for early age mental health check-ups. He believed that mental health checks should be as important for a growing adolescent as any medical check-up. He brought home the fact that if you are suffering from depression you are not abnormal, you are not a freak and there is hope in treatment. He ended his speech with the line, "Life is the hardest thing you will ever do, but it's worth it." He received a

5   zerosuicide.edc.org.

long applause, and many stood in recognition. It was a moment of many emotions.

The final speaker finished her presentation and that was our cue. The volunteers walked down and stood in a long line, bringing a visual aid to how many lives are lost to suicide each year in just Clackamas County alone. Galli then gave closing remarks and closed the program. The quiet of the crowd turned into a commotion of positive conversations all around me.

It took time to say goodbye to all the staff of Clackamas County; they were overjoyed with the turnout and the flood of positive feedback they were already receiving from the people in attendance. From what I could tell, a movement was starting but I didn't understand the magnitude.

We walked Cody out to his car and I told him I had something for him as I pulled out the envelope from Brock. Cody was puzzled. I explained what it was and could tell he was reflecting on the words I had just spoken. I asked him, knowing he wouldn't be able to give me an answer at that moment, if I could read it someday. He smiled and said he'd let me know. I gave him a hug and off he went back to college.

From the forum came an opportunity for Cody and Galli to do a broadcast on Kink Radio with Sheila Hamilton. Sheila Hamilton is an Emmy Award-Winning journalist and mental health champion. She lost her husband to suicide after he received a late diagnosis of bipolar disorder. She had recently written a book called, *All the Things We Never Knew: Chasing the Chaos of Mental Illness*. Cody shared his story and Galli talked about the forum and the work Clackamas County was doing with the gettrainedtohelp.com[6] mental health and suicide prevention training website. The conversation was gaining momentum.

In December 2015, I had the pleasure of being introduced to Sheila during a book reading organized by Clackamas County

6 https://gettrainedtohelp.com.

Behavioral Health. Sheila went on to ask me if I would be willing to do a radio broadcast with her to share my story. I was honest and said I needed to think about it and discuss it with family. I was always cautious regarding Dana – I didn't want her to feel like she always had a cloud following her. Cody was choosing the advocate walk, but that didn't mean Dana had to. She wanted me to do it, she believed in the purpose. I got back to Sheila and the show was set for January 6th, 2016.

The broadcast was a pleasant experience. I had never been on or even in a radio station, so it was a new experience all together. I was feeling the normal signs of nervous anxiety – my heart was beating fast and my palms were sweating – but I felt prepared. Prior to the broadcast, Sheila had provided an outline of questions she would be asking, so I felt as ready as I could for the interview. I have always struggled with telling my story because of the pain it may cause others whose loved ones didn't survive a suicide attempt. I was sensitive to those individuals because I was almost one of them. But knowledge is power, and the more people who became aware of mental health issues the more people could get help. I wanted to share our message of hope.

I only had to wait a short time in the lobby before Sheila came out to greet me. She could tell I was nervous and did her best to put me at ease. It wouldn't be a live show, which made it easier for me to not feel as much pressure. She grabbed some water for both of us before we entered into a smaller room with large microphones and two chairs. At this point, my nerves were really ramping up; even though I was trying to look like I was fine, I finally just confessed and told her. She was great and said all the right things to bring my confidence back. At least I wasn't trying to run out the door I just came through. I settled in my chair and just waited for her lead.

Sheila was easy to talk to, and it was just like two friends sharing life over a cup of coffee. I got emotional once or twice, but managed to keep it together, and the time passed quickly. The broadcast lasted about 30 minutes and she titled it, "We thought we had the perfect life". That was a pretty accurate title, as I truly thought we did. The broadcast would reach over 500,000 listeners via terrestrial radio.

Cody had posted his broadcast with Sheila on his Facebook page and I was trying to decide if I should post mine. I'm not much of a Facebook person, and had never posted anything about Cody's situation, but I felt that this needed to be shared – with the family's blessing, of course. I enlisted the help of one of my girlfriends to help me. The hardest part was trying to figure out what to say in the post prior to attaching the broadcast link. I noticed when I went to load the link that they didn't have the correct date of Cody's suicide attempt, but I decided to not worry about having Kink Radio correct it before posting. There were many comical moments in the technical process, but we did it. I hit post, closed my laptop and thought to myself, *Well, that was exhausting.*

The next day when I checked the post, I was overwhelmed with support and by how many people chose to share the broadcast over the internet highway. I had a number of private messages from friends who said they listened to it as a family and were grateful for the conversation that followed with their children. One mother used it as a bridge to help start the conversation with her son because she believed her son was suffering from mental illness and was fearful of bringing up the topic on her own. The broadcast allowed them, as a family, to decide to seek help. I was glad that I had taken the risk – people were being helped and I wasn't alone with my story any longer.

42
BROCK'S JOURNAL

In late January 2016, Cody let me read Brock's journal. He gave it to me after a weekend visit home. I was helping load stuff into his car before he was about to leave when he very casually handed me the envelope and said I could read it. It was so out of the blue, I wasn't prepared with any response except to say thank you. I placed it in my back jeans pocket and finished helping him carry the remaining items to his car. We said our goodbyes and did our final wave as he pulled out of the driveway. I stood there a minute to center myself. I grabbed the letter and knew that I held in my hand what I believed to be the final piece of the puzzle of what happened that night.

All of a sudden I didn't feel well, I was uncomfortable. I knew what I was about to read was something Cody and I had never talked about – the actual details of that night. Even when Cody speaks, he never goes into specific details about the method. That is not recommended by mental health professionals. It's not that I didn't know what happened, but I didn't know the intimate details. There in my hand was more information than maybe I was even prepared or ready for.

I took the envelope and placed it on the corner of my dresser where I could see it without it dominating my vision. My idea was that I'd see it daily and get used to it being there. Then, when I had the courage and was ready, it would be waiting for me.

I don't know how many days passed but, for whatever reason, I eventually grabbed the letter and the tissue box next to it, headed into the spare room and shut the door. Maybe it was because I knew I was home alone or maybe I felt emotionally stronger that day. I trusted that I was ready. I sat down in the corner of our oversized blue couch and looked at the envelope with Cody's name written in Brock's handwriting. I took out the sheet of paper and slowly unfolded it. It was just one page and typed. At first glance I thought, *Oh, this won't be so bad, it's short and I bet I can quickly read through it.* I started with the first lines and became physically ill. I had to pause and I noticed my hands starting to shake. It was like I was experiencing a scene in a movie and I just wanted to run out of the theatre. I couldn't read any further. I started crying uncontrollably, I couldn't catch my breath. I curled up on the couch and let myself feel the pain. I didn't have to be strong for anyone. I could not stop what was coming. *How can this still be in me? It's been almost three years.* The tears were flowing from some hidden caverns of pain I didn't know still existed. No longer were my body and soul able to contain them. The pain was so immense that it took me four hours to read that one page. I was a mess, but knew I needed to work through this, otherwise I would never completely move on.

It was another breakthrough for me, the final puzzle piece. As sick as I was of breakthroughs, I knew I needed to let go of the anger and let healing and hope fill that space. Problems that cause you pain can ultimately increase your hope if you let them, which was exactly what was happening all around me.

43

MY MENTAL HEALTH CHALLENGE

I added this chapter because I think it's important to bring attention to mental health issues that can arise out of medical issues, especially for women. My mental health took a turn when I had a partial hysterectomy. Very soon after the surgery I started to not feel well mentally. It took me over a month to figure out what in the hell was happening to me. My blood tests came back showing that I was right in the middle of menopause. I basically skipped pre-menopause and shot like a rocket into the middle of menopause. This isn't normally what happens, my doctor said. She started me on hormone therapy immediately, but we couldn't get the dosage correct. I was so frustrated because I was having severe mood swings. I felt anxious, couldn't sleep, having hot flushes so severe they felt like a panic attack. Once, Will thought he was going to have to take me to the Emergency Room in the middle of the night during an episode. I was gaining weight, losing weight, losing hair and having dry patches on my skin. Never in my life had I ever dealt with any of those issues and now they were compounding. I was fighting to function. I was regretting my decision to have the partial hysterectomy, but couldn't go back. The only way I could go was forward, and that scared the hell out of me. Would I be able to get my old self back? I was having anxiety about issues that had never affected me before. At times I felt spacy, like I was in the middle of an out-of-body experience. Then, at times, I felt like my old self. It was infuriating. It took over six months before I got so fed up I sought a second opinion.

My mental health was not good, and I thought I may need to go on some medication. I was on the internet reading as much as I could and researching different treatments. I wanted to feel normal again.

The new doctor immediately calmed my fears regarding the need for the surgery. It had been necessary. "If you hadn't had it when you did, your symptoms would have gotten worse and ultimately you would have needed the surgery," she told me. She understood, based on my test results, that my hormones needed to be adjusted. I had no idea how much they affected mental health. It scared me. I was angry at times because I felt I had made it to the other side regarding Cody's suicide attempt and now I was having to deal with this. I had a pity party for myself – a huge gala of a party. I also gained a greater appreciation for women who were fighting the same battle. I discovered that many women end up on an antidepressant or anxiety medication during menopause – I had had no idea.

I felt affirmed in what I knew I was feeling. I attempted different doses of hormone replacement therapy, but struggled to find the right mix. To this day, I still have to tweak my dosage and will struggle with anxiety on and off. Thankfully, it is getting better.

44

THE PHD PURSUIT –
A NEEDED SUPERPOWER

On May 16th, 2016, Cody received a Super Heart Hero award from Clackamas County for his advocate work in mental health and suicide prevention awareness. These awards are presented to community members who are doing incredible work in promoting hope, healing and recovery. The award opened up an opportunity for Cody to volunteer over the summer with Clackamas County Behavioral Health. Initially, Cody had thought about being a psychologist and doing one-on-one psychotherapy or school psychology, but after volunteering with the county, he discovered his real passion was in activism and research. For example, while volunteering he had had the opportunity to summarize and analyze best practice documents pertaining to postvention care, with a focus on local youth. Postvention care is what happens after a death by suicide to help communities and families grieve and move forward. That summary document combined public policy and research, and is currently being used when there is a death by suicide in a local community.

To pursue a career in mental health activism and research, Cody knew he would need at least a master's degree, so he arranged to take a Grad School Prep class from his advisor in the spring of 2017.

The prep class is designed to help students explore the various grad programs available and find the best fit, along with developing a personal statement. There is a massive amount of work that goes into a postgraduate application process. Cody would need to prepare and complete the following: study for and take the GRE (Graduate Record Examinations) exam, which is similar to a SAT, and receive a strong score; maintain a solid grade point average; write a personal statement (that itself took two months to complete); develop a detailed CV; and provide strong letters of recommendation. And he would need to do this all while researching and deciding on schools. He needed to submit his application by October 2017, to hit the priority deadlines for funding, and then hope he'd be selected for an interview.

Cody ended up falling into Public Health because it proved to be the best way for him to use the activism and people skills he was good at along with the behavior research abilities he was learning during his undergraduate degree. Cody soon discovered he could do far more in these areas if he had a PhD rather than a master's, so he made the decision to pursue a doctorate in Public Health with a focus on behavior health and health promotions. His overall goal was to study and help prevent youth suicide and implement broad public health changes to improve youth mental health. This was a huge shift in his academic direction and an exciting time for him.

As all of that was happening for Cody, more was happening locally on the mental health awareness front. Cody and I received a phone call from Wade, Cody's mentor from Sandy High School. Wade had taken a position at Silverton High School near Salem and they had just lost one of their senior girls to suicide. He was calling to see if Cody and I would come and share our story of hope and recovery. Cody would speak to the student population and I would present to the adult population. It would be especially difficult because it was right on the heels of the actual suicide, but we knew it was important to be timely with helpful information and we wanted to help this community move forward. This would be the first time Cody and I spoke together. It was set for May 17th, 2017.

We arrived at Silverton High School and Wade informed us that the parents of the girl who had died might attend. Cody and I both felt deep sorrow and a tremendous responsibility to do right by her. We wanted to get the message of hope out there. We knew this community was suffering.

Wade introduced us and Cody and I shared a ten-minute introduction to our story. We then broke into two groups: those who wanted to listen to Cody and those who wanted to hear me. The event was well attended and the community was grateful to hear the message. There were many questions, and I believe this was because the audience felt the freedom to talk about something they thought was taboo, because we opened the door to the topic. For some, this was the first time they had had any exposure to mental health awareness. I was grateful for all I had learned from Clackamas County Mental Health and the resources we were able to provide. The girl's parents did attend and even spoke up to affirm what I said about how invisible a person struggling with mental health can be. And this is why, no matter what, we must keep asking the questions, "How are you doing? Are you okay?"

After the presentation, a woman approached me and thanked Cody and me on behalf of the parents who lost their child. It brought me to tears and I felt their sorrow. I asked the woman to convey our love to them and to let them know they could reach out if they wanted to talk. She said she would.

Cody and I both had people around us asking questions. You could tell they were looking for hope. It was a special time for Cody and me, the first time we were both on the other side of healing. We took time to thank all the staff who had managed to quickly put the event together on such short notice. Cody and I hugged and drove our separate ways back. I was glad I had an hour's drive before I got home; I needed time to clear my head.

It was time now to focus on Dana's upcoming high school graduation. She had chosen to study business and psychology at Oregon State University. Soon both of my children would have left home, and I wasn't looking forward to it. The empty nest is a real thing. I was going to miss her. I was grateful that Cody would only be a 25-minute drive from her.

45
THE CHOICE

Cody participated in multiple online career fairs in July 2017 and was emailing professors in August to learn about research opportunities at his schools of interest and to verify they were accepting mentor students. Cody finalized the stressful process of producing his application pack and submitted it to various schools. His top three choices were the University of Arizona, the University of Wisconsin-Milwaukee and the University of North Carolina at Charlotte. Arizona and North Carolina allowed you to earn a master's concurrently as you pursued your PhD, and were tailored to students without a master's degree, so Cody felt those two schools were the best fit. Wisconsin-Milwaukee was a stand-alone PhD program which Cody wasn't sure he was ready for; but he would have been happy to get in anywhere. He had to wait until early 2018 to see if he was selected for an interview.

Dana's first term of college was rough, not academically but socially. Finding her place among her peers, finding her people, was difficult. With Cody being so close they set up another form of SOS, "Siblings on Sundays", which involved them meeting every other Sunday for lunch or dinner. Dana and Cody knew he would probably be leaving the state next year, so wanted to make the most of their time together. I was grateful for their relationship.

In December 2017, Galli reached out to Cody regarding a new opportunity with our local news station. Kathy Turner, Regional

Coordinator for Clackamas County Behavioral Health Division, had authored and compiled a 40-page Media & Mental Health Tool Kit that was being sent to local news networks to educate and spread the word about "Fair & Safe Communicating on Mental Illness & Suicide to Support Wellness & Recovery". The tool kit was designed to teach the facts about mental illness and encourage the news media to use the correct language when reporting on mental health situations, along with teaching mental health first-aid training. Clackamas County wanted as many people trained as possible – suicide was becoming an epidemic. Their research suggests that four out of five of us will have a diagnosable mental health issue in our lifetime.

The local news station wanted to do a story on this and Galli was reaching out to Cody to see if he would share his story in partnership with Galli and Kathy's message on the training. Cody was on board. The interview was in December during his winter school break. It went well and was aired on January 8th, 2018. What we didn't know was that the news station would be so moved by the segment and Cody's story that they would go on to work on a new focus. We didn't learn about that until later in the year.

It was early January when Cody started to hear from the schools he had applied to. He was excited. Wisconsin called on January 12th followed by the University of Arizona on January 17th. Both schools scheduled committee interviews via Skype for January 17th and 26th respectively. He received a rejection from Oregon Health Sciences University, which disappointed me because it was in Oregon.

Cody felt good about both interviews and both programs. He thought it would take time to hear back from them, but it didn't. Wisconsin called him the day after his interview to say they were interested in bringing him into their program and Arizona called on February 2nd, also wanting him in their program. Both would require a school visit. Cody still didn't know about funding, but to say he was freaking out nonetheless is putting it mildly.

Cody chose to rescind his applications for any master's degrees he had applied for because he was comfortable with the choices he now had in front of him. Things moved fast from there. He flew out to Milwaukee on February 15th and to Tucson, Arizona on February 26th. I had no idea which way he was leaning. He was torn – he liked aspects of each school, but still needed an offer of funding before he could make a final decision. During the wait, he heard from North Carolina that he hadn't been selected for an interview. I was rooting for the University of Arizona, closer to home and warm.

Cody got fantastic news from each school – they both offered full fellowships: Wisconsin's was for one year and Arizona's was for two years, which included non-resident tuition costs and other benefits. Given that schools only have so much funding for students, the fact that he received two full offers was fantastic. It was important for him to make his decision within a reasonable amount of time so the school he declined could offer those funds to another student.

While we all waited, Dana and I created a "Where is Cody Going?" poster to put in our kitchen. The poster had a map of the United States with each school's pennant tacked onto their state. Below was a box that said, "The Winner Is" with each school's logo pinned either side of the winner box. The plan was that when Cody had made his decision he would pin the winning logo in the winner box and wait for us to notice.

It happened one day. I walked into the kitchen and noticed it. He had pinned the Arizona logo in the winner box. I screamed with excitement. Cody and I then waited patiently until Will and finally Dana discovered the selection. It took Dana the longest, and we kind of had to nudge her along, it was good family fun. The decision was made, he was going to move to Tucson, Arizona. What a ride the last five and half years had been. This life's path was not short of winding curves.

46

PARTNERING WITH THE MEDIA –
A LAUNCHING PAD

During the first week of May 2018, the local news station got back in touch with Cody. Since his interview in January, they had made a commitment to get the word out on youth mental illness. They were doing a live town hall on May 22nd and invited him to share his story. In the United States, "town hall" events are informal public meetings around shared subjects of interest, and can be held in a range of venues. The event would be titled, "Kind is Better – Youth Mental Health". They wanted to start the conversation around the crisis with mental health and our youth. The topics would be anxiety, depression and suicide. It was to be livestreamed on Facebook, and recorded to be aired at later dates. The station was gathering together a panel of specialists, including Galli Murray from Clackamas County Behavioral Health Division. Cody was excited to be part of this program and was encouraged that the news station was building on the original interview that had aired in January. Cody called to share the news and give me a heads up that they would be contacting me to ask for my participation.

The news station reached out the next week and I agreed to be involved. I would be sharing a parent's perspective of our story and what I had learned. Whenever I step out in public situations I am nervous. I never know exactly what will be asked and that makes me uncomfortable. However, I trust the bigger picture and know these events help save lives.

Within a day or two, I was taken by surprise when an assignment editor from the news station requested an interview with me personally regarding my journey. They wanted it to air prior to the town hall – kind of like a kick off. As our story had started five years before, it showed the full journey of hope and recovery. Once the editor had described the focus of the interview – they wanted me to tell our story, share some insight on what I learned and would share with parents today, and conclude with a recap of where our family was today – I agreed. The interview was arranged for Monday, May 14th at 12pm and would air that evening. Again, things were moving fast.

The day of the interview arrived. At the very last moment, I asked my sister Elena to come along as support. I was nervous. When I talk about our story I get emotional and having her there provided comfort.

The reporter and her one-man crew arrived at our house. She was a very pleasant, professional young woman committed to getting to the heart of our story. I was impressed with the station's dedication to mental health education and awareness. The interview went smoothly and faster than I thought. They both didn't leave right away because we got to talking. I have found that whenever I talk openly about mental illness, whomever I am talking to opens up and shares their own experiences, whether it be about themselves or someone they know. Just by sharing my own story, others feel safe to share theirs. It always ends up being a healing moment for all.

The segment aired that night, and I received many texts and calls from family and friends with encouraging words about it. I was glad it went well, but also glad it was over and I could relax. Or so I thought.

47

"EXCUSE ME,
YOU'RE CALLING FROM WHERE?"

I headed to work the next day, the same as any other work day. I had a special project to complete with my co-worker Media. I was in my office upstairs at about 9:30am when my cellphone rang, and it looked like a spam call.

I looked at Media and said, jokingly, "It's a spam call, I'll put it on speaker and let's see what they want." We both laughed.

"Hello, this is Angie," I said impishly.

"Hello, this is (I don't remember his name) from the *Today* show. Am I speaking with Angie Welty?"

I looked at Media and back at my phone wide-eyed. She had put both her hands over her mouth in amazement.

"Uh, yes it is," I replied, stumbling over my words.

He continued to speak, but I wasn't comprehending his words.

I finally had to say, "Excuse me, I'm really, really sorry, but I thought you were a spam caller so I didn't listen to what your name was and why you are calling." I was scrambling to find a piece of paper and a pen to write everything down.

He laughed and re-introduced himself. I wish I could tell you his name, but it was not in any of my journal notes.

He was calling to see if there was any way my family would be willing to be on the *Today* show. They had seen my interview last night and were interested in interviewing Cody and the rest of the family for a segment they were doing about a new study out of Vanderbilt University regarding the rise in suicide attempts in our young people. They felt our family's story would be a great addition to the segment. In that nanosecond, I looked over at Media; while I had been talking, she had searched the caller's name on the internet and was giving me the thumbs up that he was legitimate. We both were shaking our heads in complete disbelief.

"Well, I'm sure we would, but are you asking us to fly to New York? Both of my children are at school," I said.

He replied, "Actually, no. We would send a producer and a camera operator to where you are. We have to do it today because they will be airing the segment tomorrow morning on the show in New York." He was hoping we could do the interview around 3pm or 4pm that day.

"Well, can I get back to you within 30 minutes? I need to ensure all of us are comfortable doing this and that we can all be together," I asked.

He said, "Absolutely. I hoped the whole family would be available for interviews."

I hung up the phone and my hands were over my mouth. What the heck was happening? Media's face was as shocked as mine. I immediately called Will. He was having a hard time believing what I was saying, but through my jumbled mess of words he understood and was able to get time off work. Next, I called Cody and Dana, going through the same drill of trying to explain what was happening. They were both in complete shock. After a few back and forth calls and emails to professors, they were able to clear their school schedules and make it home. We felt honored to be part of an amazing opportunity to spread the word nationally regarding youth mental health and suicide prevention. We didn't take what was happening lightly and felt a responsibility to do our best. We were in amazement at the speed at which things were happening.

I called back the correspondent from the *Today* show to let him know we were on board. He was grateful and let me know all the arrangements. I hung up the phone and realized there was no way I would get anything done at work that day, so I left early. Once home, I called family and friends to share the news. Shock was a common theme in our conversations.

We arranged for Cody to pick Dana up from Oregon State and leave in plenty of time to be home around 2pm. No one wanted to take any chances of having traffic issues.

I had a tremendous amount of nervous energy. I kept cleaning areas of the house I had already cleaned. It wasn't until everyone got home that I finally relaxed. We took the next hour getting ourselves ready, and then waited. It was nice to have some time before the crew arrived to sit and talk about what had transpired that morning to get us to where we were sitting.

The crew arrived on time. There was a female producer and one male camera operator. They were down to earth, personable and made us feel relaxed. After our nervous introductions, they got right to work. The camera operator walked through our downstairs spaces to find the perfect place to film. I enjoyed watching him at work. He shared how it was important to have good light and to ensure the sound came across clearly. I have a deeper appreciation for camera operators and the skills needed to ensure that you get the perfect shot, along with managing all the equipment needed to film the interview. At the same time he was scouting out a location, the producer was letting us know how the interviews would work. Cody would be the main focus of the interview, then the rest of us would be interviewed. Then we would make the famous B reel, which is supplemental footage that they took of all of us doing a family activity. For the B reel, we made some brownies. Luckily, our neighbor had eggs because I was out. The cameraman filmed us as we made the brownies and got them in the oven. He didn't know exactly what the *Today* show would end up using. As we waited for them to bake, he took footage of our family photos throughout our house. The producer then asked if I could get the actual photo files to the crew in New York.

I was sitting at my computer to gather the photo files to send to New York when I took a moment to reflect. I could smell the brownies baking in the oven and could see my family talking and laughing with the crew in our kitchen. We had all been through so much over the last few years, yet here I was sending pictures of us to be aired on the *Today* show – it was too much to emotionally take in and process. How we got to this spot was no mistake, no change of luck – I knew that to be true. It felt good to know that something wonderful was coming out of something that could have been even more tragic than it was. Cody was spreading hope to those in need, and it was a privilege to be part of that.

I brought myself back to the present and smiled as I finished getting the email ready with all the photo attachments. I still couldn't believe that it would air the next morning. The speed at which news stories moved was crazy, I had had no idea.

The *Today* crew left at about 7pm, but we didn't let them leave without brownies to go and hugs – they seemed part of our family now. As they drove away, I thought to myself, *Well, we've done our best. All we can do now is wait, along with the rest of the world, to see how it all comes together; we will have to trust the system.*

We walked inside and only had a few minutes to all talk because the kids needed to get on the road. They still had a two-hour drive back to school ahead of them. We got them on their way, and then Will and I just flopped on the couch in exhaustion. We knew none of us were going to get much sleep that night. Before heading to bed, I double-checked the video recorder to make sure it was set to record – I didn't want to mess that up.

I have said numerous times throughout this book, that every time we thought we had reached as far as we could go with our message of hope and recovery, a new door opened that we knew with complete clarity that we needed to walk through. It was as if the message had a power of its own, and would not be contained any longer. This was another example I couldn't ignore.

The phone rang at 5:30am. It was Cody, "Mom, are you up, did you see it?"

I sat up quickly, and said, "What, did it air already? We taped it!"

"Yes, you need to watch it, get up," he said excitedly.

"Well, how did it turn out? Are you happy with it?" I said, as I switched my phone to speaker so Will could hear, trying to dress at the same time. I knew Cody had been nervous about the segment because he gets concerned and sensitive about how mental illness and suicide is portrayed and communicated. He said, "Yes, I think it's good!"

Cody then shared that two of his psychology professors had already contacted him because they had heard his name on the TV as they were getting ready for work. What was crazy is that he hadn't told those professors about the interview, they just happened to see it. They told him how proud of him they were.

I couldn't wait to see how the interview had turned out. I told Cody I'd call him back as I wanted to get a hold of Dana and needed to finish getting dressed. I promised to call after we had watched it. I tried to call Dana a couple of times but had to leave voice and text messages. I couldn't remember if she would be in class or was maybe still sleeping.

Will and I rushed downstairs and loaded up the video recorder. I was trying to find within the recording where Cody's segment was. Will tried to give me a cup of coffee, but I couldn't drink it. My stomach was not cooperating and I was stressed. This was a big deal. We all felt a responsibility to do right by the mental health community and all those who have been affected by mental illness. For whatever reason, we were chosen to help push this message forward and we wanted to make sure it was done right.

Will and I sat down and watched as the NBC senior investigative and legal correspondent, Cynthia McFadden, reported the following, with contributions from Dr Greg Plemmons of Vanderbilt University:

> Doctors at Vanderbilt University looked at trends in young people thinking about or attempting suicide; in more than 115,000 cases over the past decade they found a dramatic increase.... Hospital visits for attempts or thought of suicide more than doubled, increasing by 175% between 2008 and 2015 alone. Half the cases were children between the ages of 15 and 17 years old, two-thirds of them girls. Doctors say school is playing a central role... "Rates of hospitalizations are half what they are in July what they are in October." Youth suicide rates are up 24% in the last 15 years, and researchers say suicide remains the third leading cause of death among American adolescents. The big question is why? There is no simple answer. "Some people have theorized that social media could be playing a role, that kids don't feel as connected as they used to be."[7]

As she was rolling off these statistics, I reflected and wished I had known more about mental illness five years ago, but felt so grateful that so many were hearing the news now. As the reporter introduced Cody's backstory, I could hear his laugh and see Dana mixing those brownies and Cody grabbing them out of the oven. I chuckled, thinking about the eggs.

Cody's interview started, and seeing him on national television telling his story was unreal. My eyes were glued to the television. I stared at our son, in awe of his bravery. He did what he does best, spoke from the heart, spoke truth and paid forward his message of hope. He ended his interview with this, "Depression is not a life sentence, you can get help and you can get better." He was doing what he had said he wanted

7 Excerpt from *Today*.

to do; his second chance was giving others a second chance too. The one area that I wished they would have touched on, which they didn't, was Dana's interview – the perspective of the sibling. I understand the importance of Cody's story, but I feel they missed an opportunity by not sharing her perspective. I believe that insight would have been helpful for people to hear.

Many, many grateful messages reached all of us throughout the day. Some were looking for more information. They all expressed their gratitude and some shared their own personal stories and struggles. It was obvious that the need for mental health and suicide awareness was well overdue.

Next week we still had the town hall. It was becoming more and more clear: mental health awareness and suicide prevention were on an upward trajectory, and the movement was gaining speed.

48

TOWN HALL AND SERENDIPITY

Will and I arrived at the news station after Cody. We walked up toward a gate where a woman was standing with a clipboard and a number of people were already in line to get checked in.

I noticed a gentleman walking toward us. "Hi, you must be Cody's parents," he said.

We smiled and I said, "Yes, we are, how'd you know?"

"I was the producer for Cody's interview in December, and I saw your interview. I just love your son," he said with a big smile.

He escorted us past the people in line and into a waiting room with a lot of other people who were chatting. He pointed to where Cody was standing. We thanked him and headed over to Cody. He was talking to a gentleman who he introduced as the Oregon Area Director for the American Foundation for Suicide Prevention. Cody had worked with him during his internship with Clackamas County. Galli was also there, and we were all so excited to see her; she was one of the panelists, so she wouldn't be in the audience with Cody and me. Will had decided he would prefer to watch the town hall from the outer room.

It was a packed house. The audience would include students, parents, teachers, counselors and others who had thoughts and stories to share. Cody and I had received an outline of how the evening would go, and knew they would be asking us questions to help spur conversation.

As the time for the town hall approached, they began to escort us into the studio in groups. They sat Cody and me in special seats so it would be easier for them to get to us for our interviews. We expressed to each other how we were more nervous than we had been for other interviews, since this one was to be on live television.

It is interesting watching the background work of the crew and the reporters as they prepare for a live show – there are so many moving parts. A woman came over to let us know the approximate time in the show when we would be called on for our interview, and gave us some good advice on where to stand and said not to look at the camera. I appreciated the preparation, even though it made me more nervous.

The panel consisted of one of the news anchors for the news station who would be moderating the program, along with specialists, including a professor who specialized in child and adolescent psychiatry, a clinical director who worked with anxiety patients, and Galli Murray who was a clinical social worker.

The program went off without any problems. It was great to see all these people speaking so freely about mental health, and watching the teenagers speak up about and share their stories was inspiring. The panelists provided the necessary expertise to bring facts to the table regarding mental health conditions and treatability. Cody and I did our interviews and felt they went well. We were both excited by the end of the town hall because voices had been heard and people were listening.

After the show, Cody and I went to say thank you to the news anchor and the panelists. One of the panelists asked Cody where he did his inpatient treatment; after Cody told him where, he said he believed he had been part of Cody's treatment team and had recognized him during the town hall.

Cody and I both looked at him in amazement, and I started to tear up. It was serendipitous. I hugged him. We both sincerely thanked him for helping Cody through his treatment. We took a few minutes to share stories and just talk. He was proud to see what Cody had achieved and that his treatment had been successful. I don't know how many clinicians ever get a chance to see the long-term outcomes of their patients; I'm sure it was as much a feel-good moment for him as it was for us.

As we were about ready to leave, Cody said he wanted to say goodbye to someone before he left. As we waited for him, the producer walked up to us and said, "Do you guys know the reason this town hall happened?"

I replied, "Well, I thought it was because you are focusing on youth mental health."

He smiled and said, "That's true, but it started because of Cody's story. After I did the interview with him in December, I was so moved that I came back to the station and told them we needed to do something – that's what got us started."

Will and I just stared at him, we didn't know what to say. I grinned and reached out to give him a hug as I fought back tears. I thanked him for making the commitment to move the conversation forward; we are so grateful he told us, otherwise we would never have known.

Cody found us and as we walked out to our cars, I relayed what the producer had told us. He hadn't known either, and was humbled by the story. We then headed our separate ways. I couldn't wait to call Dana on the way home and tell her about the night, even though she had been watching it on the station's Facebook page. Those are the times I wished we could all be together – I missed her.

The following week, Galli and I ended up doing a local area television show called *Afternoon Live* to round out the town hall event. And that marked the end of the television appearances for a while.

49

THAT'S A WRAP

*Five years ago today, I survived a suicide attempt. Now, I
am happier than I have ever been. Depression is not a life
sentence; if you are struggling, do not give up hope.
Your life is meaningful.*
Cody Welty, Twitter 2018

Cody graduated from college with a Bachelor's degree in
Psychology and a minor in Biology in June 2018. He received
numerous awards for his work in psychology and his leadership
on campus. He was also a finalist for the Delmer Dewey Award,
which is given to the most outstanding male graduate. His
graduation was a day of celebration on so many levels. And
Dana had made it through her freshman year at Oregon State
University and was set up with a great group of girls for off-
campus living in the next academic year.

We moved Cody to Tucson to start his PhD at the beginning
of August. Even the move to Tucson was done Welty style, with a
serious amount of craziness. We'll be reliving those stories for
a long time. Just imagine arriving at the apartment you have
rented to find it infested with bugs, so then you have to find a
new apartment and fit it out from top to bottom in the hottest
season. Add to that a broken back window on his car that had
been shipped down, and you've got some good stories.

Cody went through some serious homesickness during his first five months in Tucson. He shared with me that he was struggling mentally and emotionally, and felt it was necessary to reach out for some help. He first talked with his graduate mentor for some guidance, and through that conversation he discovered that he wasn't alone in what he was feeling. Many graduate students, especially those who relocate, struggle with missing family and friends and the familiarity of their routines, along with the added stress of graduate school. His mentor encouraged him to reach out to establish new connections and develop some consistent daily routines. Cody found a lot of comfort in that conversation, but also chose to seek out a counselor to help him maneuver through his new circumstances. Cody did focus on making additional connections outside of his classes: he joined the local rock-climbing gym, attended a running club and participated in game nights with a group of peace corps students he met in his classes. We still had our weekly Skype calls, which helped us all be involved in each other's lives and to feel more connected. It took a few weeks, but Cody started to feel better and to thrive.

In the early days of Cody's recovery I used to worry all the time about how I would handle a setback in his recovery, or a new mental health diagnosis of anyone in my family. It was a true fear for me. What I realized over time is that I was causing myself undue stress by focusing on an event that may never happen. So, instead, I focused on staying diligent in my open communication with my loved ones. I still have anxiety or concern if someone is struggling, which is normal, but now I will seek out friends, family or a professional to help me talk through the situation. I have learned to ask for help, but not without some trial and error. It took time for me to feel safe to reach out, and I'm sure it will be an area in my life that is in constant growth.

Cody and I did a few more interviews during 2019. He was asked to fly up from Tucson to be a speaker at the "Out of the Darkness Walk" put on by the American Foundation for Suicide Prevention (AFSP) at Western Oregon University, his

Alma Mater. Those AFSP events are very powerful, and I highly recommend them.

> *The American Foundation for Suicide Prevention (AFSP) is a voluntary health organization that gives those affected by suicide a nationwide community empowered by research, education, and advocacy to take action against this leading cause of death.*[8]

The news station did a follow-up town hall a year later, and asked me to come and share a few words about how all of us were doing. It was wonderful to see what had happened in a year, and all the progress that had been made in breaking down the stigma of mental health and knowing that it was no longer a taboo subject.

Cody rounded out his first year at the University of Arizona by being accepted into the Federal Summer Internship Program for Substance Abuse and Mental Health Services Administration (SAMHSA) in Rockville, Maryland. This is extremely difficult to get into, with only ten per cent of students who apply being accepted. He was fortunate enough to get to work on numerous projects related to mental illness and suicide prevention, and it was a great experience being in the heart of where policies are made.

As I wrap up editing this final chapter, it is May 2021 and we are starting to come through the Covid-19 pandemic. We have just celebrated Cody's eighth "birthday". Dana will be graduating with her college degree next month and pursuing a career in finance. I couldn't be prouder of the woman she is and will continue to become. I know that whatever she sets her mind to, great things will follow. Cody will finish his Master's program this June and will be working toward his PhD for the next two to three years. His overall goal is to become

8   Cited from https://afsp.org.

an independent investigator examining causes of adolescent suicide and developing prevention programs. He also aims to inform policy that catalyzes cultural change at the federal level. Quite the mouthful, isn't it? I'm proud of Cody, not because someday he will be referred to as Dr Welty (which we tease him about), but because of his commitment, perseverance and how he will use his title for good. One thing is for sure, you don't need a fancy title to make a change in the world – our family is evidence of that.

EPILOGUE

I am grateful for the healing process I went through in writing this book. It wasn't without painful moments. It stretched me to a point where I felt uncomfortable and sometimes just wanted to stop, but something inside me kept going. It was difficult to relive the pain. In some instances, when I interviewed those involved in our story I wasn't ready when they provided me new information and stories from their experience. That resulted in many stops and starts in writing as I had to work through that new emotional pain. I ended up putting myself back in counseling, and developed a support system of people to help me walk through this book process. I also found meditation to help calm my mind and live more in the present and not let the past take a hold of my future, but in the end our family and those involved healed even more through these words written.

There has been a common theme throughout this story, which is hope. I didn't see what was happening to Cody coming. I didn't see how our tragic day on May 1st, 2013 would unfold into the story it did. And I never saw that our family would have the privilege of being part of a youth suicide prevention and mental health movement. It must have been meant to be, because our map kept unfolding clear directions in front of us and we kept making the right turns.

It wasn't without fear, anxiety or questioning if we were doing the right thing. For me, in particular, I wasn't sure I wanted to open up and let people see our private pain. I didn't want people to know what was happening within my four walls. But putting up barriers wouldn't have helped anyone, and you wouldn't have seen the truth and beauty of recovery. I believe this book may be the final step in my journey of the promise I made to my son that night in the ER.

I often get asked what advice I would give from my experience. I would tell you not to let outward appearances fool you into thinking someone is okay. I would tell you to ask the hard questions, the uncomfortable ones, the ones that get to the heart of their feelings. Be brave, stumble over your words if necessary, but ask the questions. Ask if they struggle with sadness or have dark thoughts. Ask if they are having thoughts of suicide. Just start the conversation and be available to listen. I promise you, it gets easier to ask those questions the more you do it. Use Cody's and my broadcasts to start the conversation. You will never regret asking the questions and you could save a life. Being able to ask the questions doesn't mean you are not afraid of the response – I was and I still am, but I know there is help for me out there too. Even if you don't think you can, please ask for help.

I want to encourage you to hang on to hope. In my darkest times, I felt like I was in a pit of despair. I had sadness, pity, anger, resentment, confusion, blame and self-defeating thoughts. I evaluated and re-evaluated every element of my parenting. I knew I didn't want to stay in that pit, but the pull of those emotions was so strong. My sister, Marita, told me years later how afraid she was for me. She feared that I wouldn't be able to move on and come out the other side of the trauma. I would have to agree with her – I was also afraid. Let those closest to you help you maneuver through those uncharted emotions. Find the ones who can handle your rage and the filthy words of anger that escape through your lips into the room like thunder. Choose the ones who understand why in an instant you're sobbing so hard it brings you to your knees and you are barely able to take another breath before the next tears of emotions flow.

Find those people, seek out those professionals, and let them help to lead you out of your prison of isolation and into healing. Trauma can have an effect on the way you look at yourself, others and the world. It takes time to bring yourself back into a new normal pattern of living – give yourself time and space to heal and realize you may have setbacks and that's okay.

Our story embodied a rollercoaster ride of emotions with a front-row view. There were times I was gripping the bar for dear life and times when my arms were raised high in celebration. Our journey is still in progress, and even if I can never truly let my guard down completely, I'm okay with that. It keeps me actively aware of my own mental health and of those around me; it has become part of our common conversations. My absolute desire for this book is to provide hope, healing, inspiration and encouragement that recovery is possible. Most of all, I want everyone to start talking about mental health.

I believe that great things can happen in the midst of the most tremendous pain, even when you don't see it coming.

THANK YOU

Dana, thank you for showing me love every day through your hugs, your humor and your beautiful smile. You kept me going daily. You always stepped in and helped with whatever was needed, without question. Thank you for believing in me. You are and will always be my favorite color.

Cody, thank you for the deep conversations and for teaching me so much about mental health. Thank you for keeping it light when needed and your infamous puns. Thank you for taking all my calls for help with this book. I will always be your greatest fan.

Will, where do I start? You have seen me at my darkest moments. You sat beside me as I was in a puddle on the floor of our closet. You were by my side during all the successes. You gave me the encouragement to keep writing and dealt with my ups and downs of anxiety. I couldn't have done it without you. You fed me, kept me hydrated on various levels and listened to me read you every chapter and provided tissues when needed. Most of all, you gave me the time. I owe you a few date nights. Thank you husband, I love you.

My family, you are my foundation. Each one of you has been there for the four of us. I couldn't be more blessed to have each of you in our lives. Your love transcended all. I don't have enough words, and if I start writing them down I may not stop. Know that my heart is full from all the love, wisdom and prayers you have provided.

Marita, a special thanks to you. You never left my side. You are the epitome of what a sister's love means. You advocated for my son. You cared for my daughter. You bore the weight of my soul when I didn't have the strength to carry it. Thank you.

Elena, thank you for all of your tireless work on editing and re-editing my words on these pages. Let alone the hours of conversation to help me push this out to publishers. You helped quiet my fears. Thank you for your commitment to this book and its message. Most importantly, you have been my never-ending encourager.

Nicole and Scott, a special thanks to you both for the unmeasurable amount of time you spent caring for and loving our family. We are blessed to have you in our lives.

Jenni, thank you for the hours you spent talking on the phone and helping me work through so many different emotions. I am grateful for your friendship.

Wade, thank you for your commitment to Cody and our family. When you agreed to be his mentor, I'm sure you had no idea what you were signing up for, but you didn't even hesitate to say yes. It gave me such peace knowing you were there for Cody and our family. Thank you from the depths of my heart. You are a good human.

Bria, thank you for all the support in reading and editing this book. Your writing insight and knowledge was invaluable, along with your resources. I learned so much from you.

My friends, you were my backbone and kept me upright. You gave me the space to heal, walked with me, let me fall apart in your living rooms, checked in on me and took every phone call that came your way and sent me so many good songs to listen to and help me heal. You cared for my family, you loved us. You let me have a trucker's mouth when I needed it.

My Mt Hood Athletic Club work family, thank you all for the never-ending love and support you gave to me and my family, and for being a safe place for us all. Media, you were my comfort in the midst of my storm. Thank you.

Mom, you taught me grace, to love unconditionally and to

not judge. You taught me everyone has a story behind who they are and to be compassionate. You encouraged me to write. You showed me it was okay to write on any piece of paper I could find when an idea entered my head – I'm so glad I'm like you in that way. Thank you for laughing with me and showing me what walking in faith and forgiveness look like, I love you.

Clackamas County Behavioral Health – what an amazing team and what an amazing adventure we all took. Thank you for all you did with Cody and our family. You are rock stars for all you do for mental health. The world view of mental health and wellness is changing, one story at a time, one person at a time. Keep persevering. Galli, you're just the best – you will be part of our family forever and we are so grateful for you.

To the team at Cherish Editions, I was so nervous starting this self-publication process and wasn't sure what to expect. Each one of you was wonderful. I can't say enough about your commitment to mental health stories and education. Thank you for sharing our stories of hope.

ABOUT CHERISH EDITIONS

Cherish Editions is a bespoke self-publishing service for authors of mental health, wellbeing and inspirational books.

As a division of Trigger Publishing, the UK's leading independent mental health and wellbeing publisher, we are experienced in creating and selling positive, responsible, important and inspirational books, which work to de-stigmatize the issues around mental health and improve the mental health and wellbeing of those who read our titles.

Founded by Adam Shaw, a mental health advocate, author and philanthropist, and leading psychologist Lauren Callaghan, Cherish Editions aims to publish books that provide advice, support and inspiration. We nurture our authors so that their stories can unfurl on the page, helping them to share their uplifting and moving stories.

Cherish Editions is unique in that a percentage of the profits from the sale of our books goes directly to leading mental health charity Shawmind, to deliver its vision to provide support for those experiencing mental ill health.

Find out more about Cherish Editions by visiting cherisheditions.com or by joining us on:
Twitter @cherisheditions
Facebook @cherisheditions
Instagram @cherisheditions

Cherish
EDITIONS

ABOUT SHAWMIND

A proportion of profits from the sale of all Trigger books go to their sister charity, Shawmind, also founded by Adam Shaw and Lauren Callaghan. The charity aims to ensure that everyone has access to mental health resources whenever they need them.

You can find out more about the work Shawmind do by visiting their website: shawmind.org or joining them on:

Twitter @Shaw_Mind
Facebook @ShawmindUK
Instagram @Shaw_Mind